SEGOVIA

TRAVEL GUIDE 2024 AND BEYOND

Explore History, Culture, Cuisine, Hidden Gems and Architectural Wonders in the Heart of Spain – Packed with Detailed Maps, Travel Planner and Insider Tips

BY

JAMES W. PATRICK

Copyright © 2024 by James W. Patrick. All rights reserved. The content of this work, including but not limited to text, images, and other media, is owned by James W. Patrick and is protected under copyright laws and international agreements. No part of this work may be reproduced, shared, or transmitted in any form or by any means without the explicit written consent of James W. Patrick. Unauthorized use, duplication, or distribution of this material may lead to legal action, including both civil and criminal penalties. For permission requests or further inquiries, please reach out to the author via the contact details provided in the book or on the author's official page.

TABLE OF CONTENTS

Copyright..1
My Experience in Segovia..5
Segovia FAQ?..7
Why Visit Segovia?...9
What to Expect from this Guide..11

CHAPTER 1 INTRODUCTION TO SEGOVIA..14
1.1. Overview of Segovia..14
1.2. Historical Background..16
1.3. Climate and Best Times to Visit...18
1.4. Cultural Insights...20
1.5. Tips for First-Time Visitors...23

CHAPTER 2 ACCOMMODATION OPTIONS..26
2.1. Luxury Hotels and Paradores...26
2.2. Mid-Range Hotels and Inns..28
2.3. Budget Hostels and Guesthouses..30
2.4. Vacation Rentals and Apartments..32
2.5. Rural Accommodations and Country Houses..34

CHAPTER 3 TRANSPORTATION IN SEGOVIA..37
3.1. Navigating Segovia's Train and Bus Stations..37
3.2. Public Transportation: Buses and Taxis..39
3.3. Walking: Exploring Segovia on Foot..40
3.4. Car Rentals and Parking Tips..42
3.5. Day Trips and Regional Transportation...44

CHAPTER 4 TOP ATTRACTIONS..47
4.1. The Aqueduct of Segovia...47
4.2. Alcazar of Segovia...48
4.3. Segovia Cathedral...49
4.4. Royal Palace of La Granja de San Ildefonso...50

4.5. Walls of Segovia and City Gates.. 52

CHAPTER 5 PRACTICAL INFORMATION AND TRAVEL RESOURCES................... 54
5.1 Maps and Navigation... 54
5.2 Essential Packing List.. 56
5.3 Visa Requirements and Entry Procedures... 57
5.4 Safety Tips and Emergency Contacts.. 58
5.5 Currency, Banking, Budgeting and Money Matters................................... 60
5.6 Language, Communication and Useful Phrases....................................... 61
5.7 Useful Websites, Mobile Apps and Online Resources............................... 62
5.8 Visitor Centers and Tourist Assistance.. 63

CHAPTER 6 CULINARY DELIGHTS.. 64
6.1. Traditional Segovian Cuisine.. 64
6.2. Cochinillo Asado: Segovia's Signature Dish... 65
6.3. Tapas Bars and Local Eateries... 66
6.4. Gourmet Restaurants and Fine Dining... 68
6.5. Local Wines and Spirits.. 69

CHAPTER 7 CULTURE AND HERITAGE... 71
7.1. Roman and Medieval Heritage... 71
7.2. Museums and Cultural Institutions... 72
7.3. Religious Architecture and Monasteries... 73
7.4. Traditional Festivals and Events... 75
7.5. Arts and Crafts of Segovia... 76

CHAPTER 8 OUTDOOR ACTIVITIES AND ADVENTURES................................. 78
8.1. Hiking and Nature Trails... 78
8.2. Cycling Routes and Bike Rentals... 79
8.3. Bird Watching and Wildlife Observation... 80
8.4. Adventure Sports: Hot Air Ballooning and Paragliding............................. 81
8.5. Golf Courses and Outdoor Recreation... 82
8.6 Family and Kids Friendly Activities.. 83
8.7 Activities for Solo Travelers... 85

CHAPTER 9 SHOPPING IN SEGOVIA 87
9.1. Traditional Markets and Local Products 87
9.2. Artisanal Shops and Handcrafted Goods 89
9.3. Fashion Boutiques and Designer Stores 90
9.4. Souvenirs and Specialty Items 91
9.5. Modern Shopping Centers and Outlets 92

CHAPTER 10 DAY TRIPS AND EXCURSIONS 94
10.1. Avila: City of Saints and Stones 94
10.2. Pedraza: Medieval Village Charm 95
10.3. Sierra de Guadarrama National Park 96
10.4. El Escorial and Valley of the Fallen 97
10.5. Wine Tours in the Ribera del Duero Region 98

CHAPTER 11 ENTERTAINMENT AND NIGHTLIFE 100
11.1. Flamenco Shows and Cultural Performances 100
11.2. Bars and Pubs in the Historic Center 101
11.3. Live Music Venues and Nightclubs 103
11.4. Theatres and Cinemas 105
11.5. Seasonal Festivals and Outdoor Events 107
CONCLUSION AND INSIDER TIPS FOR VISITORS 109

SEGOVIA TRAVEL PLANNER 112

MY EXPERIENCE IN SEGOVIA

In the heart of Spain, where history whispers through the cobblestone streets and the soul of ancient tales breathes through the wind, lies a gem that has captured my heart – Segovia. As a veteran traveler and author of numerous travel guides, my journey to this enchanting city was more than just another exploration; it was a profound experience that transcended the pages of my books.

As I arrived the city, the silhouette of the iconic Alcázar against the Spanish sky welcomed me like an old friend, its turrets reaching for the heavens. It was a sight that I had seen countless times in photographs, but nothing could prepare me for the overwhelming sense of awe that washed over me in person. The Alcázar, a true architectural masterpiece, stood proudly as a testament to the rich history that unfolded within its walls.

Wandering through the narrow streets of Segovia's old town felt like stepping into a living, breathing storybook. Each corner revealed a new chapter of the city's past, with buildings adorned in intricate ironwork, vibrant flowers cascading from balconies, and locals sharing animated conversations in cozy cafes. It wasn't just the visual feast that captivated me, but the palpable sense of history that seeped through every stone, echoing tales of the past.

One cannot speak of Segovia without paying homage to its engineering marvel – the Aqueduct. As I stood before this ancient aqueduct, I marveled at the precision and ingenuity of the Roman architects who crafted this towering structure without the aid of modern technology. The sheer magnitude of the aqueduct, with its two tiers of arches stretching across the Plaza del Azoguejo, left me in awe of the ancient craftsmanship that still stood strong after centuries.

As the sun began its descent, casting a warm golden glow over the city, I made my way to the Alcázar. The interior unfolded like a treasure trove of history, each room adorned with tapestries, armor, and artifacts that transported me back in time. Standing in the

Hall of Kings, I felt a connection to the monarchs and rulers who had once walked these very halls. The view from the tower was nothing short of breathtaking, offering a panoramic spectacle of Segovia's red-tiled rooftops against the backdrop of the Sierra de Guadarrama.

To truly immerse myself in the local culture, I ventured into the bustling Plaza Mayor. The heart of social life in Segovia, this lively square was teeming with energy. Locals and visitors alike gathered at the numerous cafes and restaurants, savoring the delectable flavors of Castilian cuisine. The aroma of cochinillo (suckling pig) wafted through the air, enticing me to indulge in a culinary experience that surpassed all expectations.

Beyond the historical landmarks and gastronomic delights, it was the warmth of the people that left an indelible mark on my Segovian journey. From the passionate artisans in the workshops to the friendly locals who shared anecdotes over a glass of Rioja, every interaction felt like a glimpse into the soul of Segovia. The genuine hospitality and eagerness to share their heritage added a layer of authenticity to my experience, turning a mere visit into a heartfelt connection with the city and its people.

As I reflect on my time in Segovia, I am reminded that there are some places that transcend the boundaries of a travel guide. Segovia isn't just a destination; it's a living, breathing tapestry of stories waiting to be discovered. Whether you're an avid history enthusiast, a culinary adventurer, or simply a wanderer in search of a city with a soul, Segovia beckons with open arms, promising an experience that goes beyond the confines of words on a page.

In conclusion, my dear readers and fellow travelers, if there's one place that deserves a spot on your travel bucket list, let it be Segovia. Allow its timeless charm to weave its magic around you, and you'll find yourself not just visiting a city but becoming a part of its captivating narrative.

WHY VISIT SEGOVIA?

In the heart of Spain, lies a city that whispers tales of history, culture, architecture, and an undeniable enchantment - Segovia. In my several years of exploring the world, I have come across several wonderful destinations, but none have left an imprint on my soul quite like Segovia. Let me share with you the captivating allure of this timeless gem and why, as a wanderer at heart, you must set foot on its cobblestone streets.

Echoes of History in Every Stone

Segovia stands as a living testament to the rich tapestry of Spanish history. The moment you step into this city, you are transported to a bygone era, where each cobblestone has absorbed centuries of stories. The iconic Aqueduct of Segovia, a marvel of Roman engineering, proudly stretches across the cityscape, reminding visitors of a time when ingenuity knew no bounds. As you wander through the narrow alleys and medieval squares, the Alcázar of Segovia, a fairytale-like castle, unfolds before you, standing tall and proud against the passage of time.

A Culinary Odyssey: Savoring Segovian Delights

For a traveler, the essence of a destination is often intertwined with its culinary offerings. In Segovia, prepare your taste buds for an unforgettable journey. The city is renowned for its succulent cochinillo asado, a roasted suckling pig that has become a symbol of Segovian gastronomy. Picture yourself seated in a traditional mesón, savoring the crispy skin and tender meat, accompanied by the robust flavors of local wines. It's a culinary experience that transcends the act of eating; it becomes a celebration of Segovia's cultural identity.

Strolling Through Architectural Splendor

Segovia is a visual feast for architecture enthusiasts. Beyond the Aqueduct and Alcázar, the city is adorned with churches, monasteries, and charming plazas that paint a portrait of Spain's diverse architectural heritage. The Gothic elegance of the Segovia Cathedral, with its towering spires and intricate detailing, captivates the eye and offers a moment of reflection within its sacred walls. As you wander through the Jewish Quarter, the Casa de los Picos, adorned with its distinctive granite façade, beckons you to admire the artistry embedded in the city's architecture.

A Cultural Tapestry Unraveled: Festivals and Traditions

To truly grasp the soul of a destination, one must immerse themselves in its cultural tapestry. Segovia, with its vibrant festivals and traditions, welcomes visitors to participate in the rhythmic heartbeat of the city. The Semana Santa processions, the folkloric dances during the San Juan and San Pedro festivities, and the lively atmosphere of the local markets showcase a community deeply rooted in its traditions. It's an invitation to not just observe but to become a part of Segovia's living history.

Beyond its architectural marvels and culinary delights, Segovia's greatest charm lies in the warmth of its people. The locals, proud custodians of their city's heritage, extend a genuine hospitality that makes visitors feel not like outsiders, but as welcomed guests. Engage in conversations with the residents, let their passion for Segovia guide you, and you'll discover hidden gems and stories that no guidebook could ever capture. As a veteran traveler, I urge you to embark on a journey to Segovia. It is not just a destination; it's an odyssey through time, a feast for the senses, and an immersion into the heart of Spanish culture. Let the echoes of history, the flavors of local cuisine, the architectural wonders, and the warmth of its people be your guide. Segovia awaits!!

SEGOVIA FAQ?

1. What makes "Segovia Comprehensive Guide 2024" unique?

The guide offers up-to-date information on Segovia's attractions, dining options, accommodations, and more, ensuring a comprehensive and immersive travel experience.

2. How can I make the most of my visit to Segovia?

By using the guide's detailed itineraries, insider tips, and recommendations, you can maximize your time in Segovia and explore the city like a local.

3. Is Segovia a family-friendly destination?

Absolutely! The guide includes family-friendly activities, kid-friendly restaurants, and tips for traveling with children in Segovia.

4. Are there any hidden gems in Segovia not to be missed?

Yes, the guide highlights lesser-known attractions, off-the-beaten-path neighborhoods, and local secrets that will enhance your Segovia experience.

5. Can I find information on Segovia's history and culture in the guide?

Definitely! The guide delves into Segovia's fascinating history, cultural traditions, and must-see landmarks, providing a deeper understanding of the city's heritage.

6. How can I navigate Segovia's public transportation system?

The guide offers practical advice on using buses, taxis, and other transportation options in Segovia, making it easy for you to get around the city.

7. Are there any special events or festivals happening in Segovia in 2024?

The guide includes a calendar of events, festivals, and celebrations taking place in Segovia throughout the year, ensuring you don't miss out on any exciting happenings.

8. Can I find restaurant recommendations in the guide?

Yes, the guide features a curated list of top restaurants, bars, and cafes in Segovia, catering to all tastes and budgets.

9. What accommodation options are available in Segovia?

From luxury hotels to charming guesthouses and budget-friendly hostels, the guide covers a range of accommodation options in Segovia to suit every traveler's needs.

10. Are there any day trips from Segovia recommended in the guide?

Yes, the guide suggests day trips to nearby towns and attractions, allowing you to explore beyond Segovia and discover more of the surrounding area.

11. How can I stay safe while traveling in Segovia?

The guide provides safety tips, emergency contacts, and advice on staying vigilant and safeguarding your belongings while exploring Segovia.

12. Can I find shopping recommendations in the guide?

Yes, the guide includes shopping tips, local markets, artisanal shops, and souvenirs to buy in Segovia, ensuring you have a fulfilling shopping experience.

13. Is Segovia wheelchair accessible?

The guide offers information on accessibility options, wheelchair-friendly attractions, and accommodations to assist travelers with mobility challenges in Segovia.

14. What is the best time of year to visit Segovia?

The guide advises on the best seasons, weather conditions, and local events to help you plan your visit to Segovia at the ideal time.

15. How can I use the "Segovia Comprehensive Guide 2024 And Beyond" to enhance my travel experience?

By following the guide's tips, recommendations, maps, and suggested itineraries, you can tailor your trip to Segovia to suit your interests, preferences, and travel style.

WHAT TO EXPECT FROM THIS GUIDE

Welcome to the Segovia Comprehensive Guide, your key to unlocking the secrets of a city that stands as a testament to history, culture, and beauty. Segovia, nestled in the heart of Spain, is a city that captivates the imagination and enchants the soul. This guide is designed to provide you with an in-depth exploration of Segovia, covering all aspects of your journey, from planning and preparation to the experiences that await you. Prepare to embark on a journey through time, where every stone has a story to tell and every corner holds a new discovery.

Maps and Navigation

Our guide begins with detailed maps and navigation tools to help you orient yourself in Segovia's winding streets and historic districts. Whether you prefer a traditional paper map or a digital guide, we provide clear and concise information to ensure you can explore the city with confidence. Key landmarks, attractions, and neighborhoods are highlighted, making it easy for you to plan your route and navigate the city's treasures.

Accommodation Options

From charming bed and breakfasts to luxurious hotels, Segovia offers a range of accommodation options to suit every preference and budget. Our guide provides an overview of the best places to stay, including recommendations for romantic getaways, family-friendly lodgings, and budget-friendly hostels. We also offer tips on booking and securing the best deals for your stay in this enchanting city.

Transportation

Getting to and around Segovia is a breeze with our comprehensive transportation guide. We cover everything from arriving at Madrid's airport and taking the high-speed train to exploring the city on foot or by public transport. Learn about the most convenient and cost-effective ways to navigate Segovia, ensuring a smooth and enjoyable travel experience.

Top Attractions

Segovia is a city brimming with wonders, from the awe-inspiring Roman Aqueduct to the fairy-tale Alcázar Castle. Our guide takes you on a journey through the city's top attractions, providing historical insights, visiting tips, and must-see highlights. Discover the beauty of Segovia Cathedral, the charm of the Jewish Quarter, and the tranquility of the city's gardens and parks.

Practical Information and Travel Resources

To ensure a hassle-free trip, our guide includes essential practical information and travel resources. From currency and language tips to emergency contacts and local customs, we've got you covered. Learn about the best times to visit, what to pack, and how to stay connected with Wi-Fi and mobile data options.

Culinary Delights

Indulge in the flavors of Segovia with our guide to the city's culinary delights. From the famous cochinillo asado (roast suckling pig) to delightful tapas and sweet treats, we provide recommendations for the best dining experiences. Discover traditional restaurants, hidden gems, and food markets that offer a taste of Segovia's rich gastronomic heritage.

Culture and Heritage

Segovia's culture and heritage are woven into the fabric of the city. Our guide explores the city's museums, art galleries, and cultural institutions, offering insights into Segovia's history, art, and traditions. Learn about the city's festivals and events, where you can experience the vibrant local culture and join in the celebrations.

Outdoor Activities and Adventures

For those seeking adventure, Segovia offers a range of outdoor activities set against a backdrop of stunning landscapes. Our guide highlights the best options for hiking, cycling, and exploring the natural beauty of the surrounding areas. Discover the serene riverside walks, picturesque countryside, and opportunities for adventure sports.

Shopping

Uncover the treasures of Segovia's shopping scene, from traditional markets to boutique stores. Our guide provides tips on where to find unique souvenirs, local crafts, and fashion. Explore the city's artisan workshops, antique shops, and specialty food stores, where you can find the perfect mementos of your trip.

Day Trips and Excursions

Venture beyond Segovia with our suggestions for day trips and excursions. Explore the enchanting cities of Avila and Salamanca, the stunning landscapes of the Sierra de Guadarrama, or the royal palace of La Granja de San Ildefonso. We provide practical information on how to plan these excursions, making it easy for you to experience the diversity of the region.

Entertainment and Nightlife

Experience the vibrant nightlife of Segovia with our guide to the city's entertainment options. From traditional flamenco shows to cozy bars and lively clubs, discover the best spots to enjoy the city's nightlife. Learn about the local music scene, theaters, and cultural events that offer a glimpse into the city's artistic soul.

The **"Segovia Comprehensive Guide 2024 And Beyond"** is your gateway to the wonders of this timeless city. With detailed information, insider tips, and a passion for uncovering the heart of Segovia, this guide is your companion on a journey that promises to be unforgettable. Whether you're wandering through ancient streets, savoring culinary delights, or exploring the city's natural beauty, Segovia awaits with open arms, ready to reveal its secrets and create lasting memories.

CHAPTER 1

INTRODUCTION TO SEGOVIA

1.1. Overview of Segovia

Segovia, a city that whispers tales of a bygone era, stands as a testament to the confluence of cultures and histories that have shaped its streets, monuments, and the very essence of its being. This overview of Segovia aims to paint a vivid picture of a city that is not just a destination but a journey through time, where every cobblestone, every arch, and every vista tells a story of glory, resilience, and beauty.

A City Carved by History

Nestled in the heart of Spain, Segovia is a city that has been sculpted by the hands of time. Its history is a tapestry woven with threads of Roman ingenuity, medieval grandeur, and the artistic flourish of the Renaissance and Baroque periods. The Roman

Aqueduct, a colossal structure that stands as a testament to engineering prowess, serves as a gateway to a city where history is not just remembered but lived. Walking through the streets of Segovia is like flipping through the pages of a history book, where each chapter unfolds in the form of Gothic cathedrals, ancient synagogues, and royal palaces.

The Alcázar: A Dream Cast in Stone

Perched on a rocky crag at the city's edge, the Alcázar of Segovia is a sight to behold. With its turrets reaching for the heavens and its walls steeped in legends, the Alcázar is a castle that seems to have emerged from the realms of fairy tales. It is a symbol of the city's regal past, a fortress that has stood the test of time, witnessing the ebb and flow of empires and the march of history. Exploring the Alcázar is an experience that transports you to a time of knights and chivalry, of royal intrigues and timeless elegance.

The Cathedral: A Beacon of Gothic Splendor

The Segovia Cathedral, with its soaring spires and magnificent façade, is a masterpiece of Gothic architecture. It stands as a beacon of faith and artistry, dominating the city's skyline with its graceful presence. The cathedral's interior is a sanctuary of tranquility, with its stained glass windows casting a kaleidoscope of light on the hallowed halls. It is a place of reverence and awe, where the whispers of prayers mingle with the echoes of history.

Culinary Delights: A Taste of Tradition

Segovia's culinary landscape is a reflection of its rich heritage, offering a feast for the senses. The city is renowned for its cochinillo asado (roast suckling pig), a dish that is a celebration of flavor and tradition. Dining in Segovia is an experience that goes beyond mere sustenance; it is a journey into the heart of Castilian cuisine, where every bite tells a story of the land, its people, and their love for food.

The Jewish Quarter: A Mosaic of Cultures

The Jewish Quarter of Segovia is a testament to the city's multicultural past. With its narrow lanes and ancient buildings, it is a neighborhood that holds the memories of a community that once thrived within its walls. Exploring this quarter is an exploration of diversity and coexistence, a reminder of the city's rich tapestry of cultures and the enduring spirit of its people.

A City of Festivals: Celebrating Life and Legacy

Segovia is a city that knows how to celebrate its heritage and culture. From the vibrant festivities of the Titirimundi Puppet Festival to the solemn processions of Holy Week, the city comes alive with music, color, and joy. These festivals are not just events; they are a celebration of life and a tribute to the city's enduring legacy.

Segovia is a city that beckons with its timeless beauty and captivating history. It is a place where the past and present merge, where every corner holds a new discovery, and every moment is a brushstroke on the canvas of memory. Whether you are marveling at the Roman Aqueduct, wandering through the Alcázar, or savoring the flavors of traditional cuisine, Segovia offers an experience that is both profound and enchanting. So, embark on a journey into the heart of Segovia, where the echoes of history and the whispers of legends await to embrace you in their timeless allure.

1.2. Historical Background

Segovia, a city etched in the annals of time, stands as a silent witness to the ebb and flow of civilizations, cultures, and epochs that have shaped its very essence. The historical background of Segovia is not just a chronicle of events; it is a narrative of resilience, artistry, and the indomitable spirit of humanity. This exploration of Segovia's history aims to evoke a sense of curiosity and wonder, inviting readers to delve into the rich tapestry of a city that has been a crossroads of history.

The Dawn of Segovia: From Prehistory to the Romans

The story of Segovia begins in the mists of prehistory, with evidence of early human settlements in the surrounding areas. However, it was the Romans who left an indelible mark on the city, most notably with the construction of the awe-inspiring Aqueduct. This engineering marvel, built in the 1st century AD, was a testament to the ingenuity and ambition of the Roman Empire. It served not only as a vital water supply but also as a symbol of Roman might and civilization.

The Medieval Tapestry: Segovia Under Moorish and Christian Rule

The fall of the Roman Empire gave way to a period of Moorish rule, during which Segovia experienced a blend of cultures that enriched its social and architectural fabric. The city's strategic location made it a coveted prize, and in the 11th century, it was reconquered by Christian forces. This marked the beginning of a new chapter in Segovia's history, one that saw the city flourish as a center of trade, culture, and power. The construction of the Alcázar, a fortress that later became a royal palace, epitomized the city's medieval grandeur. The fortress stood as a sentinel, guarding the city and witnessing the ebb and flow of power, from the reign of Alfonso VI to the union of the Catholic Monarchs, Ferdinand and Isabella.

The Golden Age: Segovia in the Renaissance and Beyond

The Renaissance brought a new wave of artistic and architectural innovation to Segovia. The city became a canvas for the era's most illustrious architects and artists, who left their mark on its skyline. The Segovia Cathedral, a masterpiece of Gothic architecture, rose from the heart of the city, symbolizing both faith and the city's artistic aspirations. However, the Golden Age was not just about grandeur; it was also a time of intellectual and spiritual growth. The city's Jewish Quarter, with its synagogues and schools, was a center of learning and culture, contributing to the rich mosaic of Segovia's heritage.

The Winds of Change: Segovia Through Wars and Revolutions

The centuries that followed were marked by wars, revolutions, and the ebb of Segovia's fortunes. The War of Spanish Succession, the Peninsular War, and the Carlist Wars left their scars on the city, both physically and emotionally. However, Segovia's spirit remained unbroken, and the city continued to be a beacon of culture and history, even as it navigated the turbulent waters of change. The 20th century brought industrialization and modernization, but Segovia remained steadfast in preserving its historical legacy. The declaration of the city as a World Heritage Site by UNESCO in 1985 was a testament to its enduring significance and the global recognition of its cultural and historical treasures.

The Legacy Lives On: Segovia Today

Today, Segovia stands as a living museum, a city where the past and present coexist in harmony. The Aqueduct, the Alcázar, the Cathedral, and the winding medieval streets are not just monuments; they are the heartbeat of a city that has weathered the storms of history with grace and resilience. Visiting Segovia is not just a journey through space; it is a journey through time. It is an opportunity to walk in the footsteps of Romans, Moors, kings, and queens, to marvel at the ingenuity of ancient engineers, and to be inspired by the artistry of Renaissance masters.

The historical background of Segovia is a tapestry woven with the threads of time, a story of a city that has stood as a witness to the unfolding of human history. It is a call to the heart of history, inviting you to explore, discover, and be moved by the legacy of a city that has been a crossroads of cultures, a cradle of civilizations, and a source of inspiration for generations. So, come to Segovia, where history is not just remembered; it is lived.

1.3. Climate and Best Times to Visit

Segovia, a city etched in history and adorned with architectural marvels, is a destination that offers a unique charm in every season. Understanding the climate and identifying the best times to visit Segovia can enhance your travel experience, allowing you to immerse yourself in the city's beauty and cultural richness. This guide aims to provide a comprehensive overview of Segovia's climate and the ideal times to explore this enchanting city, stirring curiosity and excitement in the hearts of travelers.

The Tapestry of Seasons: Segovia's Climate

Segovia experiences a continental Mediterranean climate, characterized by distinct seasons that each bring their own flavor to the city. The climate is influenced by its altitude and proximity to the Sierra de Guadarrama mountains, resulting in a mix of mild and extreme weather conditions throughout the year.

Spring: A Symphony of Blossoms and Festivities

Spring in Segovia, from March to May, is a time of awakening and celebration. The city comes alive with blossoming flowers, verdant landscapes, and a gentle warmth that beckons travelers. The temperatures range from cool to mild, with average highs of 15°C (59°F) in March, 18°C (64°F) in April, and 22°C (72°F) in May.

This season is perfect for exploring the city's outdoor attractions, such as the Roman Aqueduct, the Alcázar gardens, and the tranquil parks. Spring also marks the beginning of several cultural festivals, including Holy Week (Semana Santa) and the Titirimundi Puppet Festival, offering a glimpse into Segovia's vibrant traditions.

Summer: A Time of Sunshine and Siestas

Summer, from June to August, is when Segovia basks in the warmth of the sun, with temperatures reaching highs of 28°C (82°F) in July. The days are long and sunny, providing ample opportunity to wander through the city's historic streets, enjoy outdoor dining, and experience the lively atmosphere of its plazas. However, the summer heat can be intense, especially in the afternoons. It's a time for leisurely strolls in the cooler mornings and evenings, and perhaps a siesta during the hottest part of the day. Summer also brings a host of events, including the San Juan and San Pedro festivals, filled with music, dance, and traditional celebrations.

Autumn: A Palette of Warm Hues and Cultural Richness

Autumn, from September to November, is a season of warm hues and cultural richness in Segovia. The temperatures gradually cool down, with averages ranging from 24°C (75°F) in September to 13°C (55°F) in November. The city is adorned with shades of gold and amber as the leaves change color, creating a picturesque backdrop for exploring its historical sites. This season is also a time for cultural immersion, with events like the Hay Festival Segovia, an international literary festival, and the Festival de Música Diversa, showcasing diverse musical genres. Autumn's mild weather and vibrant cultural scene make it an ideal time to visit Segovia.

Winter: A Season of Magic and Tranquility

Winter in Segovia, from December to February, is a season of magic and tranquility. The city is often blanketed in snow, transforming its landmarks into a winter wonderland. Temperatures can drop to around 3°C (37°F) in January, the coldest month, making it a cozy time to explore the city's indoor attractions, such as its museums and art galleries. The festive season brings a special charm to Segovia, with Christmas markets, nativity scenes, and traditional celebrations. It's a time for savoring local delicacies, like warm soups and roasted chestnuts, and experiencing the city's serene beauty.

Segovia is a city that offers distinct experiences in each season, from the vibrant festivities of spring and summer to the serene beauty of autumn and winter. Whether you're drawn to the cultural events, the outdoor adventures, or the tranquil moments, there's a perfect time for you to visit Segovia. As you plan your journey to this timeless city, consider what you want to experience and let the seasons guide your way. Segovia awaits with open arms, ready to reveal its wonders and create unforgettable memories in any season.

1.4. Cultural Insights

Segovia, a city steeped in history and tradition, is a cultural treasure trove that beckons travelers to delve into its rich tapestry. Beyond its iconic monuments and architectural marvels, the city is a vibrant mosaic of customs, festivities, and artistic expressions that embody the spirit of its people. This exploration of Segovia's cultural insights aims to evoke a sense of wonder and inspire travelers to immerse themselves in the unique cultural landscape of this enchanting city.

The Echoes of History: Segovia's Architectural Heritage

Segovia's cultural identity is indelibly linked to its architectural heritage, a testament to the various civilizations that have left their mark on the city. The Roman Aqueduct, a symbol of engineering prowess, stands as a reminder of the city's ancient roots. The Alcázar, with its fairy-tale silhouette, tells tales of medieval kings and queens, while the Gothic splendor of the Segovia Cathedral reflects the city's religious fervor and artistic ambition. Exploring these monuments is not just a visual experience; it's a journey through time, where each stone and spire narrates the city's storied past and its cultural evolution.

A Melting Pot of Traditions: The Festivals of Segovia

Segovia's cultural calendar is a vibrant tapestry of festivals that celebrate the city's heritage and community spirit. The Semana Santa (Holy Week) processions are a solemn and moving spectacle, showcasing the city's religious devotion. The Titirimundi Puppet Festival transforms the streets into a stage for puppeteers from around the world, delighting both young and old. The San Juan and San Pedro Fiestas in June are a time of joy and revelry, with music, dance, and traditional events that bring the city to life. These festivals are not just events; they are a window into the soul of Segovia, offering a glimpse into the customs and traditions that define the city's identity.

The Palate of Segovia: A Culinary Journey

Segovia's cuisine is a reflection of its cultural heritage, a blend of flavors that tells the story of the city's past and present. The cochinillo asado (roast suckling pig) is a culinary icon, a dish that embodies the city's gastronomic legacy. The judiones de La Granja (white beans from La Granja) and the sopa castellana (Castilian soup) are other traditional delights that offer a taste of Segovia's rustic charm. Dining in Segovia is not just about the food; it's an experience that encompasses the city's warm hospitality, the convivial atmosphere of its restaurants, and the joy of sharing a meal that is steeped in tradition and love.

The Artistic Soul of Segovia: Music, Dance, and Craftsmanship

Segovia's cultural richness extends to its music, dance, and craftsmanship, each an expression of the city's artistic soul. The city is renowned for its classical music scene, with the Segovia Music Festival attracting renowned musicians and enthusiasts from around the globe. The traditional dances, such as the jota segoviana, are a lively expression of the city's folk heritage, performed with passion and grace. The craftsmanship of Segovia is a testament to the city's artistic traditions, with skilled artisans creating exquisite ceramics, textiles, and woodwork. These crafts are not just objects; they are pieces of Segovia's cultural fabric, woven with the stories and skills of generations.

The Literary Landscape: Segovia's Stories and Poets

Segovia's cultural landscape is also enriched by its literary heritage, with the city serving as both muse and home to poets and writers. The poetry of Antonio Machado, who found inspiration in the city's beauty, captures the essence of Segovia in his verses. The city's literary tradition is celebrated through events like the Hay Festival Segovia, which brings together authors, thinkers, and readers in a celebration of ideas and storytelling.

Segovia is a city that wears its culture on its sleeve, inviting travelers to explore its traditions, savor its flavors, and revel in its artistic expressions. The cultural insights of Segovia are not just attractions; they are invitations to connect with the city's soul, to experience the warmth of its people, and to be a part of the ongoing story that is woven into the fabric of this remarkable city. So, come to Segovia, where the past and present dance together in a celebration of life, where every street, every festival, and every dish tells a tale of heritage and heart. In Segovia, culture is not just observed; it is lived, felt, and cherished.

1.5. Tips for First-Time Visitors

Welcome to Segovia, a city where history is etched into every stone and where the past whispers to those who wander its streets. As a first-time visitor to this enchanting city, you're about to embark on a journey that will take you through the annals of time, offering glimpses of Roman ingenuity, medieval grandeur, and the artistic flourishes of the Renaissance. This guide is designed to provide you with tips and insights to make your first encounter with Segovia an unforgettable experience.

Planning Your Journey: The Key to Unlocking Segovia's Wonders
Before setting foot in Segovia, a well-thought-out plan can enhance your experience and ensure that you make the most of your time. Consider the season of your visit, as each brings its own charm: the blossoming beauty of spring, the warmth of summer, the golden hues of autumn, or the serene magic of winter. Researching the city's festivals and events can also add a special dimension to your trip, allowing you to immerse yourself in the local culture and traditions.

Navigating the City: Exploring Segovia's Heart
Upon arrival, familiarize yourself with the city's layout. Segovia's compact size makes it perfect for exploring on foot, allowing you to wander through its narrow streets and discover hidden corners at your own pace. The Roman Aqueduct, an engineering marvel, is a great starting point for your exploration, leading you into the heart of the city where the Gothic Cathedral and the fairy-tale Alcázar await. Public transport and taxis are available for longer distances, but the true essence of Segovia is best experienced through leisurely strolls that reveal the city's architectural and cultural treasures.

Accommodation: Finding Your Home Away from Home
Segovia offers a range of accommodation options to suit every preference and budget. From charming bed and breakfasts nestled in historic buildings to luxurious hotels with panoramic views, the city caters to all tastes. Booking in advance is advisable, especially during peak seasons and festivals, to secure your ideal lodging and immerse yourself in the city's warm hospitality.

Culinary Delights: Savoring Segovia's Flavors

No visit to Segovia is complete without indulging in its culinary delights. The city is famed for its cochinillo asado (roast suckling pig), a dish that is a celebration of Segovian cuisine. Venture into traditional restaurants, tapas bars, and pastry shops to taste the local specialties, from savory judiones de La Granja (white beans) to sweet ponche segoviano (layered cake). Embrace the city's dining culture by taking your time to savor each meal and engaging with the locals who are always eager to share their culinary heritage.

Cultural Immersion: Experiencing the Soul of Segovia

Segovia's rich cultural tapestry is woven with history, art, and traditions. Immerse yourself in the city's heritage by visiting its museums, exploring the Alcázar's halls, and marveling at the Cathedral's Gothic splendor. Attend a classical music concert, witness a traditional festival, or simply stroll through the Jewish Quarter to feel the city's historical heartbeat.

Engage with the locals, whose stories and warmth breathe life into Segovia's stones, and you'll find that the city's true beauty lies in its people and their connection to their ancestral home.

Day Trips and Beyond: Exploring Segovia's Surroundings

While Segovia itself is a treasure trove of wonders, the surrounding region offers additional experiences that enrich your visit. Consider day trips to the nearby Royal Palace of La Granja de San Ildefonso, with its stunning gardens and fountains, or the medieval walls of Ávila. The natural beauty of the Sierra de Guadarrama National Park is also within reach, offering outdoor activities and breathtaking landscapes.

Practical Tips: Ensuring a Smooth Adventure

To ensure a smooth and enjoyable visit to Segovia, keep in mind a few practical tips:

Currency: Spain uses the Euro. Credit cards are widely accepted, but having some cash on hand is useful for smaller establishments and markets.

Language: Spanish is the official language. While many locals speak English, learning a few basic Spanish phrases can enhance your interactions and show respect for the local culture.

Safety: Segovia is generally a safe city, but as with any destination, it's wise to take standard precautions, especially in crowded areas.

As you embark on your first journey to Segovia, remember that this city is more than just a destination; it's a gateway to the past, a canvas of architectural and cultural splendor, and a place where every moment is an opportunity for discovery. Embrace the magic of Segovia, allow its history to envelop you, its flavors to delight you, and its people to welcome you into their story. Your first visit to Segovia is just the beginning of a love affair with a city that will forever hold a special place in your heart.

CHAPTER 2

ACCOMMODATION OPTIONS

Click the link or Scan the QR Code with a device to view a comprehensive map of various Accommodation Options in Segovia - https://shorturl.at/jpwG3

2.1. Luxury Hotels and Paradores

Segovia, a city that effortlessly blends historical grandeur with modern luxury, offers a selection of exquisite accommodations that promise to elevate your travel experience. From opulent hotels to majestic paradores, these establishments are not just places to stay; they are destinations in themselves, each with its own story and charm. This exploration of six luxury hotels and paradores in Segovia is designed to guide you through the city's most lavish lodging options, ensuring a stay that is both memorable and indulgent.

Parador de Segovia: A Panoramic Retreat

Perched on a hilltop overlooking the city, the Parador de Segovia offers breathtaking views of the cityscape, with the Sierra de Guadarrama as a stunning backdrop. This modern hotel seamlessly integrates contemporary design with traditional elements, providing a luxurious escape that pays homage to Segovia's heritage. Guests can indulge in amenities such as an outdoor pool, a gourmet restaurant serving local cuisine, and spacious rooms with terraces that offer panoramic vistas. Prices for a night's stay start at around €150, making it a splendid choice for those seeking a blend of luxury and scenic beauty.

Eurostars Convento Capuchinos: A Historical Haven

Nestled in the heart of the city, the Eurostars Convento Capuchinos is a 5-star hotel that has been beautifully transformed from a 16th-century convent into a haven of luxury. The hotel retains its historical charm, with original architectural features and serene cloisters, while offering modern comforts such as a spa, a fine dining restaurant, and elegantly appointed rooms. With prices starting at €180 per night, guests can experience a unique blend of history, tranquility, and opulence.

Hotel Real Segovia: Elegance in the City Center

Located in the vibrant heart of Segovia, Hotel Real Segovia is a stylish and elegant hotel that offers a perfect base for exploring the city's attractions. The hotel boasts chic and comfortable rooms, a rooftop terrace with stunning views of the Cathedral, and a cozy lounge bar. Guests can enjoy a blend of contemporary amenities and classic charm, with prices starting at €120 per night. Hotel Real Segovia is an ideal choice for travelers seeking luxury and convenience in the city center.

Hotel Palacio San Facundo: A Regal Retreat

Set in a beautifully restored 16th-century palace, Hotel Palacio San Facundo combines regal elegance with modern luxury. Located just a stone's throw from the Plaza Mayor, this boutique hotel features a charming courtyard, sophisticated rooms, and a stylish café-bar. The hotel's tranquil ambiance and attentive service make it a perfect sanctuary for relaxation after a day of exploring Segovia. Prices for a night's stay begin at €130, offering guests a royal experience in the heart of the city.

Hotel Don Felipe: A Modern Gem with Historic Charm

Hotel Don Felipe is a contemporary hotel that is situated within the historic quarter of Segovia, offering easy access to the Alcázar and other landmarks. The hotel's sleek design is complemented by its warm and welcoming atmosphere, with amenities such as a rooftop terrace, a garden, and tastefully decorated rooms. Guests can enjoy a comfortable and stylish stay, with prices starting at €100 per night, making Hotel Don Felipe a great choice for those seeking modern luxury in a historic setting.

Parador de La Granja: A Royal Escape

Located in the nearby town of La Granja de San Ildefonso, the Parador de La Granja is a luxurious retreat set in an 18th-century royal palace. Surrounded by beautiful gardens and the stunning landscapes of the Sierra de Guadarrama, this parador offers a regal experience with its opulent rooms, a spa, and a restaurant serving exquisite local cuisine. Prices for a night's stay start at around €160, providing guests with a taste of royal life in a serene and picturesque setting.

Segovia's luxury hotels and paradores offer more than just accommodations; they offer an experience that intertwines the city's rich history with modern indulgence. Whether you choose to stay in a panoramic parador, a historical convent, or a regal palace, these establishments promise to provide a stay that is as memorable as it is luxurious. As you embark on your journey to Segovia, let these hotels and paradores be your gateway to a world of elegance, comfort, and unforgettable experiences.

2.2. Mid-Range Hotels and Inns

Segovia, a city that captivates with its historic allure and timeless beauty, offers a variety of accommodation options that cater to travelers seeking comfort and charm without the opulence of luxury hotels. Mid-range hotels and inns in Segovia provide a perfect balance of cozy ambiance, convenient amenities, and affordability. This guide delves into six such establishments, each with its own unique character, ensuring a pleasant and memorable stay in this enchanting city.

Hotel Infanta Isabel: A Gem in the Heart of the City

Located in the bustling Plaza Mayor, Hotel Infanta Isabel is a mid-range hotel that boasts an enviable position with stunning views of the Segovia Cathedral. The hotel's classic décor, combined with modern comforts, creates a welcoming atmosphere for guests. With prices starting at around €80 per night, visitors can enjoy amenities such as air-conditioned rooms, free Wi-Fi, and an on-site café. The hotel's central location makes it an ideal base for exploring Segovia's historic sites and vibrant street life.

Hospedaje San Francisco: A Blend of History and Comfort

Situated in a renovated 16th-century building, Hospedaje San Francisco offers a unique stay with a historical backdrop. Located just a short walk from the Aqueduct, this mid-range inn provides cozy accommodations with prices starting at €60 per night. Guests can enjoy comfortable rooms, a charming courtyard, and the convenience of being close to Segovia's main attractions. The inn's blend of history and comfort makes it a popular choice for travelers seeking an authentic Segovian experience.

Hotel Condes de Castilla: A Modern Retreat in a Historic Setting

Hotel Condes de Castilla is set in a beautifully restored 13th-century building, offering a mix of contemporary amenities and historic charm. Located near the Plaza Mayor, the hotel features stylish rooms, a rooftop terrace with panoramic views, and a cozy bar. With prices starting at €70 per night, guests can enjoy a comfortable stay in a prime location, with easy access to Segovia's cultural landmarks and dining options.

La Casa Mudéjar Hospedería: A Cultural Encounter

La Casa Mudéjar Hospedería is a mid-range hotel that stands out for its unique Mudéjar-style architecture and art collection. Situated in the historic center, close to the Cathedral, the hotel offers rooms starting at €75 per night. Guests can explore the on-site museum, relax in the spa, and savor local cuisine at the restaurant. The hotel's commitment to preserving Segovia's cultural heritage makes it an appealing choice for those interested in history and art.

Hotel Acueducto: A View to Remember

Overlooking the iconic Roman Aqueduct, Hotel Acueducto provides guests with a memorable vista at an affordable price, with rooms starting at €65 per night. The hotel features comfortable accommodations, a terrace with aqueduct views, and a convenient location for exploring the city on foot. The proximity to Segovia's ancient masterpiece and the value for money make Hotel Acueducto a favored option for budget-conscious travelers.

Hostal Segovia: A Cozy Hideaway

Nestled in a quiet street near the Alcázar, Hostal Segovia offers a peaceful retreat with a homely atmosphere. With prices starting at €50 per night, this mid-range inn provides simple yet comfortable rooms, a delightful garden, and personalized service. The hostal's tranquil setting and friendly staff ensure a relaxing stay, making it an ideal choice for those seeking a quiet escape in the heart of Segovia.

Segovia's mid-range hotels and inns offer a wonderful opportunity to experience the city's charm and history without compromising on comfort or breaking the bank. Each of these establishments provides a unique perspective on Segovia, from panoramic views of ancient monuments to stays in historic buildings. As you plan your visit to this captivating city, consider these mid-range options for a stay that combines affordability with the enchanting essence of Segovia.

2.3. Budget Hostels and Guesthouses

Segovia, a city that enchants with its historic splendor and timeless charm, is also a destination that caters to travelers on a budget. For those seeking affordable accommodations without sacrificing comfort and convenience, Segovia offers a selection of budget hostels and guesthouses. Each of these establishments provides a unique and cost-effective way to experience the city, ensuring that your stay in Segovia is both memorable and wallet-friendly.

Hostal Plaza: A Cozy Retreat in the City Center

Nestled in the heart of Segovia, just a stone's throw from the Plaza Mayor, Hostal Plaza offers a warm and welcoming atmosphere at an affordable price. With rates starting at around €40 per night, guests can enjoy comfortable rooms, complimentary Wi-Fi, and the convenience of being within walking distance of major attractions like the Segovia Cathedral and the Aqueduct. The hostal's central location and friendly service make it an ideal choice for budget-conscious travelers seeking to explore the city's wonders.

Hospedaje Bar El Gato: A Budget-Friendly Gem

Located near the iconic Aqueduct, Hospedaje Bar El Gato is a budget hostel that offers a unique blend of affordability and comfort. With prices starting at €35 per night, guests can enjoy simple yet cozy rooms, a lively bar on the ground floor, and easy access to Segovia's historic sites. The hospedaje's laid-back atmosphere and proximity to local eateries and bars make it a popular choice for backpackers and young travelers looking to experience Segovia's vibrant culture.

La Huerta de San Lorenzo: A Tranquil Escape

Situated in a quiet area close to the city center, La Huerta de San Lorenzo is a charming guesthouse that provides a peaceful retreat for budget travelers. With rates starting at €45 per night, guests can enjoy rustic-style rooms, a beautiful garden, and a vegetarian restaurant on-site. The guesthouse's serene ambiance and commitment to sustainable living offer a unique and eco-friendly lodging option in Segovia.

Hostal Don Jaime: Comfort and Convenience

Hostal Don Jaime, located near the Aqueduct, offers budget-friendly accommodations with a focus on comfort and convenience. With prices starting at €40 per night, guests can enjoy clean and comfortable rooms, free Wi-Fi, and a prime location for exploring Segovia's historic center. The hostal's friendly staff and excellent value make it a great option for travelers looking to make the most of their stay in Segovia without breaking the bank.

Pension Odeon: A Homely Haven

Pension Odeon, situated in the heart of Segovia, provides a homely and budget-friendly lodging option for visitors. With rates starting at €35 per night, guests can enjoy simple yet comfortable rooms, a shared kitchen for preparing meals, and a cozy lounge area. The pension's welcoming atmosphere and convenient location near the Plaza Mayor make it an excellent choice for travelers seeking an affordable and authentic Segovian experience.

Hostal Segovia: A Blend of Tradition and Value

Hostal Segovia, located in the historic quarter of the city, offers a blend of tradition and value for budget-conscious travelers. With prices starting at €45 per night, guests can enjoy traditionally decorated rooms, a picturesque courtyard, and easy access to Segovia's main attractions. The hostal's combination of historic charm and modern amenities makes it a great option for those looking to experience the city's heritage without spending a fortune.

Segovia's budget hostels and guesthouses provide an array of options for travelers seeking to explore this captivating city without overspending. Each of these establishments offers a unique perspective on Segovia, from its central plazas to its tranquil gardens, all while providing comfort and convenience at an affordable price. As you plan your journey to Segovia, consider these budget-friendly accommodations for a stay that is both enriching and economical.

2.4. Vacation Rentals and Apartments

Segovia, a city that weaves together the threads of history, culture, and architectural beauty, offers travelers the opportunity to immerse themselves in its charm through a variety of vacation rentals and apartments. These accommodations provide a more intimate and personalized experience, allowing visitors to live like locals and enjoy the comforts of home while exploring this enchanting city. This guide delves into six distinct vacation rentals and apartments in Segovia, each offering a unique blend of amenities, location, and character.

Casa de la Moneda Apartment: A Riverside Retreat

Nestled along the banks of the Eresma River, Casa de la Moneda Apartment offers a tranquil escape with stunning views of the Alcázar and the surrounding countryside. This charming apartment features elegant décor, a fully equipped kitchen, and a cozy living area. With prices starting at €100 per night, guests can enjoy the serenity of the riverside while being just a short walk from Segovia's historic center. The apartment's unique location and picturesque setting make it an ideal choice for those seeking a peaceful yet convenient stay.

Aqueduct View Apartment: A Historical Panorama

Situated in the heart of the city, the Aqueduct View Apartment offers breathtaking views of Segovia's iconic Roman Aqueduct. This modern apartment is priced from €120 per night and boasts contemporary furnishings, a spacious living area, and a well-appointed kitchen. The floor-to-ceiling windows provide an unparalleled panorama of the ancient structure, allowing guests to marvel at this architectural wonder from the comfort of their living room. The apartment's central location makes it a perfect base for exploring the city's attractions and enjoying its vibrant atmosphere.

Alcázar Garden Apartment: A Royal Neighbor

Located just steps away from the majestic Alcázar, the Alcázar Garden Apartment is a cozy retreat that offers a unique perspective on one of Segovia's most famous landmarks. With prices starting at €90 per night, this apartment features a quaint garden, traditional décor, and all the necessary amenities for a comfortable stay. The proximity to the Alcázar and the old town allows guests to immerse themselves in Segovia's historical charm and easily access its cultural treasures.

Plaza Mayor Loft: Urban Elegance

Overlooking the bustling Plaza Mayor, the Plaza Mayor Loft is a stylish urban apartment that combines modern elegance with historic charm. Priced from €110 per night, the loft offers an open-plan living space, chic furnishings, and a fully equipped kitchen. The balcony provides a front-row seat to the lively square below, where guests can observe the daily life of Segovia and partake in its festive atmosphere. The loft's central location is ideal for those looking to experience the city's vibrant urban culture.

La Muralla Studio: A Cozy Hideaway

Tucked away in a quiet corner near the city walls, La Muralla Studio is a charming and affordable option for travelers. With prices starting at €70 per night, this cozy studio offers a comfortable living space, a kitchenette, and a private patio. The studio's intimate setting and rustic décor provide a warm and welcoming atmosphere, making it a perfect hideaway for couples or solo travelers seeking a peaceful retreat in the heart of Segovia.

Casa del Pintor: An Artistic Abode

Casa del Pintor, located in the picturesque Jewish Quarter, is a beautifully restored apartment that once served as an artist's studio. Priced from €95 per night, this apartment features original artwork, a spacious living area, and a well-equipped kitchen. The blend of artistic flair and historical ambiance creates a unique and inspiring environment for guests. The apartment's location in the Jewish Quarter offers a glimpse into Segovia's diverse cultural heritage and provides easy access to the city's landmarks and hidden gems.

Vacation rentals and apartments in Segovia offer travelers a chance to experience the city's enchanting allure in a more personal and intimate setting. Whether you're seeking a riverside retreat, a historical panorama, or an artistic abode, these accommodations provide the comforts of home while allowing you to immerse yourself in the beauty and culture of Segovia. As you plan your visit to this captivating city, consider these vacation rentals and apartments for a stay that combines convenience, character, and a touch of local charm.

2.5. Rural Accommodations and Country Houses

Segovia, a city renowned for its historical grandeur and architectural marvels, is surrounded by a countryside that offers a different kind of charm. The rural accommodations and country houses near Segovia provide a serene escape into nature, where the rustic beauty of the landscape blends seamlessly with the comfort and hospitality of these unique retreats. This guide explores seven such rural accommodations, each offering a distinctive experience for travelers seeking tranquility and a connection with the natural beauty of the Segovian countryside.

La Casa Vieja: A Rustic Retreat

Nestled in the quaint village of Tabanera del Monte, La Casa Vieja is a charming rural house that embodies the essence of traditional Spanish countryside living. With rates starting at €90 per night, this cozy accommodation features exposed wooden beams, stone walls, and a warm fireplace, creating an inviting atmosphere. Guests can enjoy the tranquility of the surrounding gardens, savor home-cooked meals, and explore the nearby pine forests and hiking trails.

El Mirador del Alcázar: Panoramic Perfection

Perched on a hill with stunning views of the Segovia Alcázar and the Sierra de Guadarrama, El Mirador del Alcázar is a country house that offers a picturesque retreat. Priced from €100 per night, this accommodation boasts spacious rooms, a large terrace, and a garden where guests can relax and soak in the breathtaking scenery. The house's prime location allows for easy access to outdoor activities such as cycling, horse riding, and bird watching.

Casa Rural Los Barreros: A Homely Haven

Located in the charming village of San Cristóbal de Segovia, Casa Rural Los Barreros is a delightful country house that provides a home-away-from-home experience. With prices starting at €80 per night, guests can enjoy comfortable accommodations, a fully equipped kitchen, and a cozy living area. The house's proximity to Segovia city and the natural parks makes it an ideal base for exploring both cultural landmarks and the great outdoors.

Finca La Casona: An Elegant Estate

Finca La Casona, situated in the serene countryside of Espirdo, is an elegant estate that combines luxury with rural charm. Starting at €120 per night, this country house offers beautifully appointed rooms, a swimming pool, and extensive gardens. Guests can indulge in gourmet meals prepared with locally sourced ingredients, partake in wine tasting sessions, and enjoy leisurely walks in the surrounding countryside.

El Zaguán de Cabanillas: A Traditional Hideaway

El Zaguán de Cabanillas is a traditional rural house located in the peaceful village of Cabanillas del Monte. Priced from €85 per night, this accommodation features rustic décor, a fireplace, and a patio with a barbecue area. The house provides a tranquil setting for relaxation and is a perfect starting point for hiking and exploring the nearby natural reserves.

La Fuente del Poval: A Countryside Oasis

Nestled in the heart of the countryside, La Fuente del Poval is a country house that offers a serene oasis away from the hustle and bustle of city life. With rates starting at €95 per night, guests can enjoy spacious accommodations, a garden with a swimming pool, and stunning views of the surrounding fields and forests. The house's location in the village of Caballar provides easy access to Segovia and the opportunity to experience rural life in a traditional Spanish village.

Casa del Plantel: A Garden Retreat

Casa del Plantel, located in the picturesque village of La Lastrilla, is a rural accommodation that boasts a beautiful garden and a peaceful ambiance. Starting at €75 per night, this country house offers comfortable rooms, a communal kitchen, and a lounge area. Guests can unwind in the garden, enjoy outdoor dining, and explore the nearby walking trails and historic sites.

The rural accommodations and country houses near Segovia offer a unique opportunity to experience the tranquility and beauty of the Spanish countryside. Each of these establishments provides a warm welcome, comfortable amenities, and a chance to connect with nature and local culture. Whether you're seeking a rustic retreat, an elegant estate, or a traditional hideaway, these rural accommodations promise a memorable and relaxing stay in the enchanting surroundings of Segovia.

CHAPTER 3

TRANSPORTATION IN SEGOVIA

3.1. Navigating Segovia's Train and Bus Stations

As one ventures into the enchanting city of Segovia, nestled in the heart of Spain's Castile and León region, the journey is often as memorable as the destination itself. The city's train and bus stations serve as gateways to its historic streets and architectural marvels, offering visitors a seamless transition from travel to exploration. Understanding the nuances of navigating these transportation hubs can significantly enhance the experience, allowing travelers to immerse themselves in the beauty and culture of Segovia with ease. The Segovia-Guiomar Train Station, a modern facility located about 4 kilometers from the city center, stands as a testament to the blend of contemporary convenience and historical charm that characterizes Segovia. Despite its distance from the old town, the station is well-connected, with frequent bus services and taxis readily available to whisk visitors to the heart of the city. Inside, travelers are greeted with a range of amenities, including ticket offices, waiting areas, restrooms, and a small café to relax and refuel. The station serves as a key stop on the high-speed AVE line, connecting Segovia to Madrid and other major cities in Spain, making it a popular choice for those seeking a swift and comfortable journey.

For those arriving by bus, the Segovia Bus Station offers a different but equally convenient gateway to the city. Located closer to the historic center, the bus station is just a short walk from the iconic Roman Aqueduct, providing an immediate immersion into Segovia's rich history. The station itself is equipped with a ticket office, waiting area, restrooms, and a small café. Buses from various parts of Spain, including Madrid, Valladolid, and Salamanca, converge here, making it a bustling hub of activity and a meeting point for travelers from all walks of life. Navigating these stations is made easier by the helpful signage and information desks, where visitors can inquire about schedules, routes, and local attractions. Both the train and bus stations are designed with accessibility in mind, ensuring that travelers with mobility challenges can move around comfortably. For those looking to explore the surrounding region, car rental services are available near the train station, offering the freedom to venture beyond the city limits at one's own pace.

One unique feature of Segovia's train station is its integration with the city's public transportation system. The Line 11 bus, for example, provides a direct link between the Segovia-Guiomar Train Station and the Aqueduct, making it a convenient option for those looking to dive straight into sightseeing. Additionally, the bus station's central location makes it an ideal starting point for exploring the city on foot, with many of Segovia's famous landmarks, including the Alcázar and the Cathedral, just a stroll away. In conclusion, navigating the train and bus stations in Segovia is a straightforward and pleasant experience, thanks to the well-organized facilities and the array of services available to travelers. Whether arriving by train or bus, visitors can look forward to a warm welcome and a smooth transition into the captivating world of Segovia, where history and modernity coexist in harmony. With a little planning and an adventurous spirit, the journey through Segovia's transportation hubs can be the first chapter in an unforgettable exploration of this timeless Spanish city.

3.2. Public Transportation: Buses and Taxis

Segovia, a city steeped in history and architectural beauty, offers a range of public transportation options that make exploring its wonders both convenient and efficient. From the winding streets of the old town to the panoramic views of the surrounding countryside, the city's buses and taxis provide accessible means for visitors to discover Segovia's many facets. This guide delves into the details of Segovia's public transportation systems, providing essential information for travelers seeking to navigate the city with ease.

Buses: The Pulse of Segovia's Transport

The bus system in Segovia is operated by Urbanos de Segovia, offering a network of routes that cover the city and its suburbs. The buses are a reliable and cost-effective way to travel, with routes connecting major landmarks, residential areas, and commercial zones. The main bus station, Estación de Autobuses de Segovia, serves as a hub for both urban and intercity services. Fares for urban buses are affordable, with a single ticket costing around €1.00. Visitors can also opt for a bono-bus card, a rechargeable card that offers discounted fares for multiple trips. The buses run at regular intervals throughout the day, with schedules available at bus stops and online. For those looking to explore beyond the city, intercity buses connect Segovia to nearby towns and attractions, providing an opportunity to discover the region's diverse landscapes and cultural offerings.

Taxis: A Convenient Option for Personalized Travel

Taxis in Segovia offer a convenient and flexible mode of transportation, ideal for those seeking a more personalized travel experience. Taxi stands are located at strategic points throughout the city, including the train station, the bus station, and the main square, Plaza Mayor. Taxis can also be hailed on the street or booked in advance by phone or through taxi service apps. The fare for taxis in Segovia is metered, with a starting rate and an additional charge per kilometer. Prices may vary depending on the time of day, with higher rates typically applied at night and on weekends. For visitors traveling to or from the Madrid-Barajas Airport, pre-arranged taxi services offer fixed rates, providing a hassle-free option for airport transfers.

Accessibility and Convenience: Ensuring a Smooth Journey

Segovia's public transportation is designed to cater to the needs of all travelers, including those with mobility challenges. Many buses are equipped with low-floor access and dedicated spaces for wheelchairs, ensuring a comfortable and accessible journey. Taxis in Segovia are also required to provide accessible services upon request, with some vehicles specially adapted for passengers with disabilities. For visitors seeking information on routes, schedules, and fares, the Segovia Tourism Office and the official websites of Urbanos de Segovia and local taxi services provide up-to-date details and assistance. Additionally, mobile apps and online maps can be valuable tools for planning your trips and navigating the city's public transportation network.

Segovia's buses and taxis offer an efficient and accessible way to explore the city's rich tapestry of history, culture, and natural beauty. Whether you're wandering through the ancient streets of the old town, marveling at the Roman Aqueduct, or venturing into the surrounding countryside, the city's public transportation provides a seamless and enjoyable travel experience. By embracing the convenience and accessibility of Segovia's buses and taxis, visitors can immerse themselves in the enchanting world of this historic city, creating memories that will last a lifetime.

3.3. Walking: Exploring Segovia on Foot

Segovia, a city that unfolds like a historical tapestry, is best experienced at a leisurely pace, with each step revealing a new layer of its rich past. Walking through Segovia is not just a mode of transportation; it's an invitation to immerse oneself in the city's architectural wonders, vibrant culture, and the stories etched into its stones. This guide is dedicated to exploring Segovia on foot, offering insights into how to navigate its streets and uncover its secrets, one step at a time.

The Heartbeat of Segovia: The Old Town

The Old Town of Segovia is a pedestrian's paradise, with its narrow cobblestone streets, hidden courtyards, and picturesque squares. The journey begins at the iconic Roman Aqueduct, a marvel of ancient engineering that serves as the gateway to the city's historic center. From there, a leisurely stroll along Calle Real leads to the Plaza Mayor, the bustling heart of Segovia, where the grand Segovia Cathedral stands as a testament to Gothic splendor. Exploring the Old Town on foot allows visitors to appreciate the intricate details of Segovia's architecture, from the ornate facades of its buildings to the wrought-iron balconies adorned with flowers. It's an opportunity to pause, look up, and marvel at the beauty that surrounds you.

A Walk Through History: Segovia's Landmarks

Walking through Segovia is akin to taking a step back in time. As you wander, you'll encounter landmarks that tell the story of the city's past. The Alcázar of Segovia, perched on a rocky outcrop, is a highlight of any walking tour. This fairy-tale castle, with its towers and battlements, offers panoramic views of the surrounding countryside and a glimpse into the lives of the royalty who once resided there. Other must-see sights on your walking journey include the medieval walls that encircle the city, the Jewish Quarter with its narrow alleys and ancient synagogues, and the Monastery of San Antonio el Real, with its exquisite Mudéjar architecture.

The Green Side of Segovia: Parks and Gardens

Segovia's charm extends beyond its historic buildings to its green spaces, where nature and history intertwine. The Alcázar's gardens are a tranquil oasis, perfect for a leisurely stroll amidst manicured hedges and vibrant flower beds. For a more expansive natural escape, the Parque del Alcázar offers walking paths that wind through wooded areas and offer stunning views of the fortress. Just outside the city, the Royal Palace of La Granja de San Ildefonso boasts expansive gardens in the French style, with fountains, sculptures, and meticulously designed landscapes. It's a short journey from Segovia and an ideal destination for a leisurely day spent walking in the footsteps of kings.

Practical Tips for Walking in Segovia

Walking in Segovia is an enjoyable and straightforward way to explore the city. Comfortable footwear is a must, as the cobblestone streets can be uneven. Be sure to carry water, especially during the warmer months, and take breaks in the city's many plazas and cafes to rest and soak in the atmosphere. For those looking to delve deeper into Segovia's history, guided walking tours are available, offering expert insights into the city's landmarks and hidden gems. These tours provide a deeper understanding of Segovia's cultural and historical context, enriching your walking experience.

Exploring Segovia on foot is an invitation to slow down and savor the city's timeless beauty. It's an opportunity to connect with its history, immerse yourself in its culture, and discover the stories that lie around every corner. Whether you're wandering through the Old Town, admiring its landmarks, or strolling through its gardens, walking in Segovia is a journey that engages all the senses. So, take a step forward, and let the magic of Segovia unfold before you, one step at a time.

3.4. Car Rentals and Parking Tips

Segovia, a city renowned for its historical marvels and picturesque landscapes, offers a unique experience for visitors who choose to explore its wonders by car. Renting a car provides the freedom to discover Segovia and its surrounding areas at your own pace, allowing for spontaneous detours and immersive exploration. This guide aims to provide detailed information on car rentals and parking tips in Segovia, ensuring a smooth and enjoyable journey through this captivating city.

Car Rentals: Your Gateway to Segovia's Wonders

Renting a car in Segovia is a convenient option for travelers looking to venture beyond the city's historic center and explore the broader region. Several reputable car rental agencies operate in Segovia, including well-known international brands and local providers. Rental offices are typically located near the train station, the city center, or can be found at Madrid-Barajas Airport for those arriving by air.

Prices for car rentals vary depending on the type of vehicle, rental duration, and the time of year. On average, rates start at around €30 per day for a compact car, with options available for larger vehicles or luxury models at higher prices. It's advisable to book your rental car in advance, especially during peak tourist seasons, to secure the best rates and availability.

When renting a car, ensure that you have a valid driver's license, a credit card for the deposit, and appropriate insurance coverage. Familiarize yourself with local traffic regulations and consider opting for a GPS navigation system to help navigate the winding roads and historic streets of Segovia.

Parking Tips: Navigating Segovia with Ease

Parking in Segovia can be a challenge, especially in the historic center where streets are narrow and parking spaces are limited. However, several options are available to ensure a hassle-free experience:

1. Blue Zones (Zona Azul): These are paid parking zones located throughout the city, marked by blue lines. Parking in these zones is typically limited to a maximum duration, with rates ranging from €1 to €2 per hour. Pay-and-display machines are available for purchasing tickets, and parking is often free during lunch hours and on Sundays.

2. Parking Lots and Garages: Segovia offers several public parking lots and garages, providing a secure option for leaving your car while exploring the city. Notable parking facilities include the Parking de la Catedral, Parking Acueducto, and Parking José Zorrilla. Prices vary, with daily rates averaging around €15 to €20.

3. Park and Ride (P+R): For those staying outside the city center, park and ride facilities offer a convenient solution. You can park your car in designated areas on the outskirts of the city and use public transportation to reach the historic center. This option is cost-effective and helps avoid the congestion of central Segovia.

4. Street Parking: In residential areas and outside the city center, street parking may be available free of charge. However, be mindful of parking regulations and restrictions to avoid fines.

Renting a car and navigating parking in Segovia opens up a world of possibilities for exploring this enchanting city and its surroundings. With the freedom to travel at your own pace, you can uncover hidden gems, venture into the countryside, and experience the full beauty of Segovia and beyond. By planning ahead and following these tips, your car rental and parking experience in Segovia can be both convenient and enjoyable, adding another memorable chapter to your travel story.

3.5. Day Trips and Regional Transportation

Segovia, a city of timeless beauty and historical wonder, serves as a perfect base for exploring the rich cultural and natural landscapes of the surrounding region. Day trips from Segovia offer a chance to discover the diverse attractions that lie within easy reach, from medieval towns to natural parks. This guide provides an extensive overview of day trips and regional transportation options, ensuring that visitors can seamlessly venture beyond Segovia to uncover the treasures of the area.

The Royal Palace of La Granja de San Ildefonso: A Baroque Masterpiece
Just a short drive from Segovia, the Royal Palace of La Granja de San Ildefonso is a stunning example of Spanish Baroque architecture, set amidst beautifully landscaped gardens with impressive fountains. The palace, often referred to as the "Spanish Versailles," is accessible by local bus services such as La Sepulvedana, with tickets priced at around €2-€4. The journey takes approximately 30 minutes, making it an ideal half-day excursion.

The Walled City of Ávila: A UNESCO World Heritage Site
Ávila, known for its well-preserved medieval walls, is another must-visit destination. Located about an hour's drive from Segovia, this historic city can be reached by intercity buses or trains. The train journey from Segovia's Guiomar Station to Ávila takes around

30-40 minutes, with prices starting at €6. Once there, visitors can explore the ancient walls, the Cathedral of Ávila, and the Convent of Saint Teresa.

The Roman Aqueduct of Segovia: A Marvel of Ancient Engineering

While not a day trip, no visit to Segovia is complete without witnessing the awe-inspiring Roman Aqueduct. This ancient structure, one of the best-preserved in the world, is a testament to Roman engineering and a symbol of Segovia's rich history. The aqueduct is easily accessible on foot from the city center, and there is no cost to admire this magnificent monument.

Pedraza: A Medieval Village

Pedraza, a charming medieval village, is located about 37 kilometers from Segovia. Known for its cobblestone streets and historic architecture, Pedraza offers a glimpse into Spain's past. Accessible by car or local bus services, this picturesque village is perfect for a leisurely day trip. Visitors can explore the Castle of Pedraza, the Plaza Mayor, and enjoy the local cuisine in one of the village's quaint restaurants.

The Sierra de Guadarrama National Park: A Natural Escape

For nature enthusiasts, the Sierra de Guadarrama National Park is a must-visit. Located approximately 30 kilometers from Segovia, the park offers a range of outdoor activities, including hiking, bird watching, and skiing in the winter months. The park is accessible by car or local bus services, providing an opportunity to experience the natural beauty of the region.

The Enchanting Town of Sepúlveda and the Hoces del Río Duratón Natural Park

Sepúlveda, a picturesque town known for its Romanesque churches and traditional cuisine, is a gateway to the Hoces del Río Duratón Natural Park. The park, with its dramatic canyons and river landscapes, is ideal for hiking, canoeing, and bird watching. Visitors can take a bus from Segovia to Sepúlveda, with the journey taking around an hour.

Day trips from Segovia offer a chance to explore the diverse cultural and natural attractions of the surrounding region. Whether you're drawn to the architectural splendor of the Royal Palace of La Granja de San Ildefonso, the medieval charm of Ávila and Pedraza, or the natural beauty of the Sierra de Guadarrama National Park, the region around Segovia is replete with destinations that enrich the travel experience. With convenient regional transportation options, these day trips are easily accessible, allowing visitors to immerse themselves in the history, culture, and natural wonders that lie beyond the city of Segovia.

CHAPTER 4

TOP ATTRACTIONS

Click the link or Scan the QR Code with a device to view a comprehensive map of Top Attractions in Segovia - https://shorturl.at/rsFR2

4.1. The Aqueduct of Segovia

The Aqueduct of Segovia is not just an iconic symbol of the city but also a testament to the engineering prowess of the ancient Romans. This magnificent structure, dating back to the 1st or 2nd century AD, has stood the test of time and continues to leave visitors in awe of its grandeur and historical significance. Located at the heart of Segovia, the aqueduct is impossible to miss. It spans from the city's outskirts, near the Plaza del Azoguejo, and stretches majestically across the landscape. The most impressive section, often featured in photographs and postcards, consists of 166 arches, reaching a maximum height of 28.5 meters. The entire aqueduct is built from massive granite blocks, ingeniously fitted together without the use of mortar, showcasing the remarkable skill and precision of its builders.

Visitors to Segovia are often struck by the sheer size and beauty of the aqueduct. It's a popular spot for taking photographs, and many choose to start their exploration of the city from this point. The Plaza del Azoguejo, located at the base of the aqueduct, is a bustling square where you can find cafes, souvenir shops, and restaurants. It's a great place to sit and admire the view of the aqueduct while enjoying a cup of coffee or a traditional Spanish meal. One of the unique features of the Aqueduct of Segovia is its remarkable state of preservation. Despite being nearly two thousand years old, the aqueduct has survived largely intact, thanks in part to the careful maintenance and restoration efforts over the centuries. It was used to carry water from the Frio River to the city until the mid-19th century, a testament to its enduring functionality.

For those interested in learning more about the history and construction of the aqueduct, there are guided tours available. These tours provide fascinating insights into the Roman engineering techniques, the historical context of the aqueduct, and its significance to the city of Segovia. In addition to its historical and architectural appeal, the Aqueduct of Segovia also plays a role in the city's cultural events. It serves as a backdrop for various festivals and celebrations throughout the year, adding to the vibrant atmosphere of Segovia.

Overall, the Aqueduct of Segovia is a must-visit landmark for anyone traveling to the city. Its awe-inspiring presence, historical importance, and central location make it a focal point for tourists and a symbol of Segovia's rich heritage. Whether you're interested in history, and architecture, or simply looking for a picturesque spot to relax and soak in the local culture, the aqueduct offers a memorable experience for all visitors.

4.2. Alcazar of Segovia

The Alcazar of Segovia is a majestic fortress that stands proudly on a rocky outcrop at the confluence of two rivers, the Eresma and the Clamores. This iconic castle, with its distinctive shape resembling the bow of a ship, has been a symbol of Segovia's rich history and architectural splendor for centuries. Its strategic location offers breathtaking views of the surrounding landscape, making it a must-visit destination for travelers exploring the city. The origins of the Alcazar date back to the early 12th century, though it has undergone numerous transformations over the years. Initially serving as a fortress, the Alcazar has also been a royal palace, a state prison, and a military academy throughout its history. Today, it stands as a museum and a testament to the architectural and cultural heritage of Spain.

One of the most striking features of the Alcazar is its architecture, which showcases a blend of Romanesque, Gothic, and Mudéjar styles. The exterior of the castle is characterized by its imposing walls, crenelated battlements, and robust towers. The most famous of these towers is the Torre del Homenaje, which offers panoramic views of Segovia and its surroundings. Visitors can climb to the top of the tower to experience the stunning vistas that have captivated people for centuries. Inside the Alcazar, the opulent rooms and halls are adorned with intricate decorations, tapestries, and armor. The Throne Room, with its ornate ceiling and regal furnishings, is a highlight, as is the Hall of the Kings, which features a frieze depicting 52 statues of Spanish monarchs. The castle's interior also houses an extensive collection of medieval weaponry, providing insight into the military history of the region. The Alcazar's strategic position overlooking the city also played a crucial role in Segovia's defense system. The castle's fortifications were designed to protect the city from invaders, and its elevated location allowed for early detection of approaching armies. Today, visitors can explore the castle's ramparts and walk along the walls to appreciate the defensive architecture that has stood the test of time.

For those interested in learning more about the Alcazar's history and significance, guided tours are available. These tours provide valuable insights into the castle's past, its architectural features, and its role in Spanish history. Additionally, the Alcazar often hosts temporary exhibitions and cultural events, making it a lively and dynamic place to visit. In conclusion, the Alcazar of Segovia is a remarkable landmark that offers a glimpse into the rich tapestry of Spain's history. Its architectural beauty, strategic importance, and cultural significance make it an essential stop for anyone visiting Segovia. Whether you're exploring its grand halls, admiring the views from its towers, or delving into its storied past, the Alcazar is sure to leave a lasting impression.

4.3. Segovia Cathedral

Segovia Cathedral, often referred to as the "Lady of the Cathedrals," is a magnificent example of Gothic architecture that dominates the skyline of the historic city of Segovia. Located in the main square, Plaza Mayor, the cathedral is not only a religious landmark but also an architectural masterpiece that draws visitors from around the world. Construction of Segovia Cathedral began in the early 16th century, after the previous cathedral was destroyed during a revolt. The cathedral was designed by the architect Juan Gil de Hontañón and is considered one of the last great Gothic cathedrals built in

Spain. Its towering spires, intricate façades, and stunning stained glass windows are a testament to the craftsmanship and artistry of the period. One of the unique features of Segovia Cathedral is its location. Unlike many cathedrals that are built on the highest point of a city, Segovia Cathedral is situated in the heart of the city, surrounded by the bustling activity of the Plaza Mayor. This central location makes it an integral part of daily life in Segovia and a focal point for visitors and locals alike.

Upon entering the cathedral, visitors are greeted by a vast interior filled with light, soaring columns, and exquisite chapels. The main altar, with its impressive altarpiece, is a highlight, showcasing the work of renowned artists such as Juan de Juni and Francisco Giralte. The cathedral also boasts a beautiful cloister, which provides a tranquil space for reflection away from the hustle and bustle of the city. One of the most remarkable aspects of Segovia Cathedral is its collection of art and religious artifacts. The cathedral museum houses an array of treasures, including tapestries, sculptures, and paintings, some of which date back to the 14th century. The choir stalls, carved from walnut wood, are particularly noteworthy for their intricate detail and craftsmanship. For those interested in exploring the cathedral further, guided tours are available. These tours offer insights into the history, architecture, and art of the cathedral, providing a deeper understanding of its significance. Additionally, visitors can climb the tower for panoramic views of Segovia and the surrounding countryside, a breathtaking experience that should not be missed.

In conclusion, Segovia Cathedral is a jewel in the crown of this historic city. Its architectural beauty, rich history, and cultural significance make it a must-visit destination for anyone traveling to Segovia. Whether you are admiring its exterior from the plaza, exploring its art-filled interior, or taking in the views from the tower, Segovia Cathedral is sure to leave a lasting impression.

4.4. Royal Palace of La Granja de San Ildefonso

The Royal Palace of La Granja de San Ildefonso, often simply referred to as La Granja, is a splendid example of Spanish Baroque architecture and a testament to the opulence of 18th-century royal life. Located in the town of San Ildefonso, just 11 kilometers from the city of Segovia, this palace and its gardens are a magnificent sight that transports visitors back in time to an era of grandeur and elegance. Originally built as a summer retreat for King Philip V, the first Spanish Bourbon king, La Granja was inspired by the grandeur of the Palace of Versailles in France. The king wanted a palace that would rival the French court's splendor, and indeed, La Granja is often referred to as the "Versailles of Spain." The palace was designed by the architect Teodoro Ardemans, and construction began in the early 18th century. Over the years, subsequent monarchs added their touches, enhancing its beauty and opulence. One of the most striking features of La Granja is its stunning gardens, which cover over 146 hectares. These gardens are a masterpiece of landscape design, featuring meticulously manicured hedges, elaborate sculptures, and a series of spectacular fountains. The fountains, which are among the best examples of 18th-century hydraulic engineering, are an absolute highlight. They depict various mythological scenes and are known for their grandeur and the intricacy of their design. The Fountain of Neptune, the Baths of Diana, and the Fountain of the Fame are particularly noteworthy. On special occasions, the fountains are set in motion, creating a breathtaking display of water and artistry.

The interior of the palace is equally impressive, with a series of lavishly decorated rooms that showcase the luxury of royal life. The Hall of the Halberdiers, with its stunning frescoes and elaborate stucco work, is a standout. The Royal Chapel, with its exquisite altarpiece, and the Throne Room, adorned with rich tapestries and gilded decorations, are also must-see spaces. The palace also houses an important collection of artworks, including paintings, sculptures, and tapestries, many of which were commissioned by the royal family. Visitors to La Granja can also explore the Royal Glass Factory, located nearby. This historic factory was established to supply the palace with glass and crystal, and today it serves as a museum showcasing the art of glassmaking, with live demonstrations and a collection of beautiful glass pieces. In conclusion, the Royal Palace of La Granja de San Ildefonso is a jewel in the crown of Segovia's cultural heritage. Its magnificent gardens, stunning fountains, and opulent interiors make it a must-visit destination for anyone interested in history, architecture, and the arts. A visit to La Granja offers a glimpse into the splendor of Spain's royal past and is an experience that is sure to leave a lasting impression.

4.5. Walls of Segovia and City Gates

The Walls of Segovia and its City Gates are a testament to the city's rich history and strategic importance throughout the centuries. These ancient fortifications, which date back to the Roman era and were expanded during the Middle Ages, encircle the old city, serving as a protective barrier and a symbol of Segovia's enduring strength. The walls of Segovia stretch for approximately three kilometers, following the contours of the city's rocky outcrop. They are punctuated by a series of towers and gates, each with its own story to tell. Walking along the walls offers a unique perspective on the city, providing glimpses of its historic buildings, narrow streets, and the surrounding landscape. One of the most notable gates is the Puerta de San Andrés, located in the Jewish Quarter. This gate is particularly interesting because it houses the Centro Didáctico de la Judería, a center dedicated to the history and culture of Segovia's Jewish community. Visitors can learn about the significant role that Jews played in the city's history and the architectural and cultural legacy they left behind.

Another important gate is the Puerta del Sol, which was part of the city's medieval expansion. This gate is characterized by its pointed arch and the remnants of a drawbridge mechanism, giving visitors a sense of the defensive measures that were once in place. Near the Puerta del Sol, one can also find the Casa de los Picos, a Renaissance building known for its façade adorned with diamond-shaped stones. The Puerta de San Cebrián, located near the Alcázar, is another significant entrance to the city. This gate offers stunning views of the surrounding countryside and the Eresma River, making it a popular spot for photographs. It also provides easy access to some of Segovia's most iconic landmarks, including the Alcázar and the nearby Monastery of San Antonio el Real.

For those interested in exploring the walls in more depth, guided tours are available. These tours provide insights into the construction, history, and significance of the walls and gates, offering a deeper understanding of Segovia's past. Additionally, some sections of the walls are accessible for walking, allowing visitors to experience the fortifications up close and enjoy panoramic views of the city. In conclusion, the Walls of Segovia and its City Gates are not only important historical structures but also integral parts of the city's identity. They offer a fascinating glimpse into Segovia's past, from its Roman foundations to its medieval expansions. Exploring these ancient fortifications is an essential experience for anyone visiting Segovia, providing a unique connection to the city's history and a different perspective on its present.

CHAPTER 5

PRACTICAL INFORMATION AND TRAVEL RESOURCES

Click the link or Scan the QR Code with a device to view a comprehensive map of Segovia – *https://shorturl.at/doDY6*

5.1 Maps and Navigation

Segovia, a city steeped in history and culture, is a treasure trove of architectural marvels and culinary delights. As an experienced traveler and author of travel guides, I understand the importance of having a detailed guide to navigating this enchanting city. This essay aims to provide an extensive overview of maps and navigation in Segovia, covering essential landmarks, hotels, hidden gems, shopping centers, restaurants, and bars, along with navigation tips and practical information to ensure a memorable experience for visitors.

Essential Landmarks: The Pillars of Segovia

Segovia's skyline is dominated by its iconic landmarks, each with its own story. The Roman Aqueduct, an engineering marvel, serves as a gateway to the city's rich past. The Alcázar of Segovia, perched on a rocky outcrop, is a fairy-tale castle that offers panoramic views and a glimpse into medieval times. The Segovia Cathedral, with its soaring Gothic spires, stands as a testament to the city's religious and architectural heritage.

Accommodations: A Place to Rest

Segovia offers a range of accommodations to suit every taste and budget. For a luxurious stay, the Parador de Segovia provides modern amenities with stunning views of the city. Mid-range options like Hotel Don Felipe and Hotel Condes de Castilla offer comfort and convenience, while budget travelers can find cozy lodgings at Hostal Plaza and Hospedaje Bar El Gato.

Hidden Gems: Exploring Segovia's Secrets

Beyond the well-known attractions, Segovia hides several gems waiting to be discovered. The Casa de los Picos, with its façade adorned with diamond-shaped stones, is a unique architectural wonder. The Church of San Millán, one of the oldest in the city, showcases a blend of Romanesque and Moorish styles. The Mirador de la Pradera de San Marcos offers a tranquil spot with breathtaking views of the Alcázar.

Shopping Centers: A Shopper's Delight

Segovia's shopping scene is a blend of traditional and modern. The Old Town is filled with artisan shops selling ceramics, jewelry, and leather goods. For local food products, the Mercado de la Plaza Mayor offers a variety of cheeses, meats, and sweets. For a more contemporary shopping experience, the Luz de Castilla Shopping Center provides a range of retail stores and eateries.

Restaurants and Bars: A Culinary Journey

Segovia's culinary landscape is as diverse as its history. Mesón de Cándido, located near the Aqueduct, is famous for its traditional cochinillo asado (roast suckling pig). Restaurante José María offers a blend of classic and contemporary Castilian cuisine. For a casual dining experience, La Concepción serves delicious tapas and local dishes. Wine enthusiasts can enjoy a glass of Ribera del Duero at La Taberna Rubi.

Navigation Tips and Directions

Navigating Segovia is best done on foot, as the city's compact size and pedestrian-friendly streets make it easy to explore. A detailed map or a GPS-enabled smartphone app is essential for finding your way around. For longer distances, local buses operated by Urbanos de Segovia provide convenient transportation. The city's main landmarks, such as the Aqueduct and the Alcázar, are well-signposted and serve as reference points for orientation.

Practical Information: Enhancing Your Visit

When exploring Segovia, comfortable walking shoes are a must, as the city's cobblestone streets and hilly terrain can be challenging. Carrying a reusable water bottle is advisable, as there are several public fountains with drinkable water. For museum visits and cultural sites, it's recommended to check opening hours and ticket prices in advance. The Segovia Tourist Card offers discounts and access to various attractions, making it a valuable resource for visitors.

Segovia is a city that invites exploration, with its winding streets, historic landmarks, and vibrant culinary scene. By utilizing maps and navigation tools, staying informed about accommodations and dining options, and uncovering hidden gems, visitors can fully immerse themselves in the beauty and culture of Segovia. Whether you're marveling at the ancient Aqueduct, savoring a plate of cochinillo asado, or simply wandering through the Old Town, Segovia promises an unforgettable journey through the heart of Spain's rich history and heritage.

5.2 Essential Packing List

When planning a trip to Segovia, packing appropriately can make all the difference in ensuring a comfortable and enjoyable visit. This historic city, known for its stunning architecture and rich cultural heritage, offers a range of experiences, from exploring ancient landmarks to savoring local cuisine. Here's a guide to help you pack the essentials for your Segovia adventure. First and foremost, comfortable footwear is a must. Segovia's cobblestone streets and hilly terrain require sturdy shoes that can handle walking and exploring. Whether you're strolling along the Aqueduct or climbing the steps to the Alcázar, your feet will thank you for choosing supportive and comfortable shoes.

The weather in Segovia can vary, so it's wise to pack layers. Even in the warmer months, the evenings can be cool, especially if you're out enjoying the city's vibrant nightlife. A lightweight jacket or sweater that can easily be carried in a daypack is a good idea. In the cooler months, a warm coat, scarf, and gloves are essential to keep you cozy while wandering through the city's enchanting streets. As you'll likely be spending a lot of time outdoors, sun protection is important. A hat, sunglasses, and sunscreen will protect you from the sun's rays, especially during the summer when the sun can be quite strong. Even in the cooler months, it's a good idea to have sunscreen on hand for sunny days.

For capturing the beauty of Segovia, don't forget your camera or smartphone. The city is filled with picturesque scenes, from the iconic Aqueduct to the fairy-tale Alcázar. A portable charger can also be handy to ensure your devices stay powered throughout the day. A reusable water bottle is a practical item to include in your packing list. There are several public fountains around the city where you can refill your bottle, staying hydrated as you explore. When it comes to clothing, casual and comfortable is the way to go. Segovia has a relaxed atmosphere, so there's no need for formal attire. However, if you plan on dining at one of the city's finer restaurants or attending a cultural event, you might want to pack a smart-casual outfit. Lastly, a small backpack or crossbody bag is ideal for carrying your essentials as you roam the city. Make sure it's secure and easy to carry, as you'll want your hands free to take photos, consult your map, or enjoy a delicious cone of helado (ice cream).

Packing for Segovia is all about comfort, practicality, and being prepared for the city's diverse experiences. With the right items in your suitcase, you'll be ready to immerse yourself in the charm and history of this beautiful Spanish city.

5.3 Visa Requirements and Entry Procedures

Traveling to Segovia, a historic city in Spain, requires an understanding of the visa requirements and entry procedures that apply to Spain as a whole. As Segovia is part of the Schengen Area, the visa requirements and entry procedures are consistent with those of other Schengen countries. For visitors from countries that are part of the visa-exempt program, such as the United States, Canada, Australia, and Japan, among others, no visa is required for stays of up to 90 days within a 180-day period. However, it's important to ensure that your passport is valid for at least three months beyond your planned departure date from the Schengen Area. If you are a citizen of a country that does require a visa to enter Spain and the Schengen Area, you will need to apply for a Schengen visa. This visa allows you to travel freely within the Schengen Area for up to 90 days within a 180-day period. To apply for a Schengen visa, you will need to submit an application to the nearest Spanish consulate or embassy in your home country, along with the required documents, which typically include a valid passport, proof of accommodation, travel itinerary, travel insurance, and proof of financial means.

Upon arrival in Spain, whether you need a visa or not, you will go through passport control where you may be asked to present your travel documents, including your passport and, if applicable, your visa. You may also be asked to show proof of accommodation, such as a hotel reservation or an invitation letter if you are staying with friends or family, and evidence of sufficient funds for your stay. It's also important to note that as of 2022, the European Union plans to implement the European Travel Information and Authorization System (ETIAS), which will require visa-exempt travelers to obtain travel authorization before entering the Schengen Area. This system is similar to the ESTA system used by the United States. Travelers will need to apply for ETIAS authorization online before their trip.

In conclusion, when planning a trip to Segovia, it's essential to check the latest visa requirements and entry procedures for Spain. By ensuring that you have the necessary travel documents and meet the entry requirements, you can look forward to a smooth and enjoyable visit to this beautiful and historic city.

5.4 Safety Tips and Emergency Contacts

Traveling to Segovia, a city renowned for its historical charm and architectural beauty, is generally considered safe for visitors. However, like any travel destination, it's important to be aware of safety tips and have emergency contact information handy to ensure a worry-free and enjoyable experience. One of the primary safety tips for travelers in Segovia is to be mindful of personal belongings, especially in crowded areas such as the vicinity of the Aqueduct, Plaza Mayor, and other tourist attractions. Pickpocketing can occur in busy spots, so it's advisable to keep valuables secure and close to your body. Using a money belt or a crossbody bag with a zippered closure can help protect your possessions.

When exploring the city, it's a good idea to stay on well-lit, populated streets, especially at night. While Segovia is generally safe, avoiding isolated areas after dark can further reduce any risks. If you're unsure about the safety of a particular area, don't hesitate to ask locals or hotel staff for advice. For those who plan to drive in Segovia, be aware of local traffic laws and parking regulations. The city's narrow, winding streets and limited parking can be challenging for drivers. It's often more convenient to park outside the city center and explore on foot or use public transportation. In case of an emergency, it's crucial to know the relevant contact numbers. The general emergency number in Spain is 112, which can be dialed for immediate assistance from police, fire services, or medical teams. For non-urgent medical attention, you can visit the Segovia Hospital (Hospital General de Segovia) located at Carretera de Ávila, s/n, 40002 Segovia.

If you need to contact the police for non-emergency matters, such as reporting a lost item, the local police station (Policía Local) is situated at Calle de San Agustín, 23, 40001 Segovia. For tourist-related inquiries or assistance, the Segovia Tourist Office, located near the Aqueduct at Plaza del Azoguejo, 1, can provide helpful information and support. It's also a good idea to have the contact information of your home country's embassy or consulate in Spain readily available. In case of lost passports or other serious issues, they can provide necessary assistance and guidance.

In conclusion, Segovia is a delightful and safe city to visit, with its rich history and stunning architecture offering a memorable experience. By taking basic precautions, staying aware of your surroundings, and having important emergency contacts at hand, you can ensure a secure and enjoyable trip to this beautiful Spanish city.

5.5 Currency, Banking, Budgeting and Money Matters

Traveling to Segovia, a captivating city in Spain, requires some understanding of the local currency, banking options, and budgeting tips to ensure a smooth and enjoyable experience. Managing money matters effectively can enhance your visit, allowing you to focus on the city's rich history and stunning architecture. The currency used in Segovia, as in the rest of Spain, is the Euro (€). It's advisable to have some cash on hand for small purchases, such as snacks, souvenirs, or tickets for local transportation. However, credit and debit cards are widely accepted in most restaurants, hotels, and shops. It's a good idea to inform your bank of your travel plans to avoid any issues with card usage abroad.

For currency exchange, it's generally recommended to do so before arriving in Segovia, as exchange rates offered in the city may not be as favorable. If you need to exchange money while in Segovia, you can find exchange services at banks or at the post office (Correos), located at Calle de los Coches, 2. Keep in mind that banks in Spain typically operate from Monday to Friday, with limited hours, usually from 8:30 am to 2:00 pm. ATMs are readily available throughout Segovia, particularly near tourist areas and in the city center. They offer a convenient way to withdraw cash in Euros. Be aware of any fees charged by your bank for international ATM withdrawals and check for any partnership networks that might reduce these fees.

Budgeting for your trip to Segovia depends on your travel style and preferences. Accommodation costs can vary, with options ranging from budget-friendly hostels to luxurious hotels. Dining out in Segovia can be a delightful experience, with a variety of restaurants catering to different budgets. To save money, consider having your main meal at lunchtime, when many restaurants offer a "menú del día" – a set menu at a reasonable price. When it comes to sightseeing, many of Segovia's attractions, such as the Aqueduct and the Jewish Quarter, can be explored for free. However, some sites, like the Alcázar and the Cathedral, have entrance fees. Investing in a Segovia tourist card or a combined ticket for multiple attractions can offer savings if you plan to visit several paid sites.

In conclusion, handling money matters in Segovia involves a mix of planning and flexibility. By familiarizing yourself with the local currency, understanding banking options, and budgeting according to your needs, you can ensure a hassle-free and enjoyable visit to this enchanting Spanish city.

5.7 Useful Websites, Mobile Apps and Online Resources

In today's digital age, having access to useful websites, mobile apps, and online resources can greatly enhance your travel experience in Segovia. These tools can provide valuable information, assist with navigation, and offer insights into the city's attractions, making your visit more enjoyable and efficient. One essential website for anyone planning a trip to Segovia is the official tourism website of the city, www.turismodesegovia.com. This site offers a wealth of information, including details about Segovia's landmarks, cultural events, guided tours, and accommodation options. It's a great starting point for planning your itinerary and learning about the city's rich history and offerings.

For navigating the city and exploring its attractions, Google Maps is an indispensable app. It provides detailed maps, walking directions, and information about points of interest. Additionally, the app can help you find nearby restaurants, shops, and other amenities, making it easier to navigate the city's streets and discover hidden gems. If you're interested in learning more about Segovia's history and architecture while you explore, consider downloading audio guide apps such as Rick Steves Audio Europe or VoiceMap. These apps offer self-guided walking tours that provide insights into the city's landmarks, including the Aqueduct, the Alcázar, and the Cathedral.

For public transportation information, the official website of Segovia's bus service, www.urbanosdesegovia.com, is a useful resource. It provides schedules, routes, and fare information for the city's bus network, helping you plan your journeys around Segovia and its surrounding areas. When it comes to dining, apps like TripAdvisor and Yelp can be helpful for finding restaurants in Segovia. These platforms offer user reviews, ratings, and photos, allowing you to discover popular eateries and local favorites. For reservations, apps like ElTenedor (TheFork) offer a convenient way to book tables at many restaurants in the city.

For those interested in cultural events and activities, the Segovia Cultura Habitada website, www.segoviaculturahabitada.es, provides information about concerts, exhibitions, theater performances, and other events happening in the city. It's a great way to stay updated on Segovia's vibrant cultural scene during your visit.

In conclusion, leveraging websites, mobile apps, and online resources can significantly enhance your travel experience in Segovia. By utilizing these tools, you can access a wealth of information at your fingertips, making it easier to plan your trip, navigate the city, and immerse yourself in the rich culture and history of this beautiful Spanish destination.

5.8 Visitor Centers and Tourist Assistance

Segovia, a city steeped in history and culture, offers a range of visitor centers and tourist assistance services to ensure that visitors have a memorable and hassle-free experience. These centers provide valuable information, guidance, and support to help you make the most of your time in this enchanting city. One of the main visitor centers in Segovia is the Centro de Recepción de Visitantes, located near the iconic Aqueduct at Plaza del Azoguejo, 1. This center is a vital resource for tourists, offering a wide range of services including free maps, brochures, and information about guided tours, attractions, events, and accommodations. The friendly staff can assist you with any queries you may have and provide recommendations tailored to your interests. The center also has a gift shop where you can purchase souvenirs and local products.

Another important visitor center is the Oficina de Turismo de Segovia, situated in the historic Casa de los Picos at Calle Juan Bravo, 33. This office is housed in a Renaissance building known for its façade adorned with diamond-shaped stones. Here, you can find information about Segovia's cultural heritage, landmarks, and walking routes. The staff can also help you with booking guided tours and provide tips on how to explore the city's hidden gems. For those interested in exploring Segovia's Jewish heritage, the Centro Didáctico de la Judería, located at Calle de la Judería Vieja, 12, is a must-visit. This center offers insights into the history and contributions of the Jewish community in Segovia. You can learn about the city's Jewish Quarter, its synagogues, and the cultural legacy of this important community.

In addition to these centers, Segovia has several tourist information points strategically located throughout the city, including near the Cathedral and the Alcázar. These points provide quick access to maps, brochures, and basic information, making it easy for visitors to find their way around and discover the city's attractions. For those seeking personalized assistance or facing any difficulties during their visit, the tourist office also offers a helpline that can be reached by phone or email. The staff is equipped to handle a range of inquiries, from accommodation issues to lost property, ensuring that visitors have a support system throughout their stay in Segovia.

In conclusion, Segovia's visitor centers and tourist assistance services play a crucial role in enhancing the visitor experience. By offering a wealth of information, guidance, and support, these centers ensure that tourists can fully immerse themselves in the beauty and history of this remarkable city, making their visit an unforgettable journey.

CHAPTER 6

CULINARY DELIGHTS

6.1. Traditional Segovian Cuisine

Segovia, a city renowned for its rich history and architectural splendor, is also a haven for gastronomic delights. The traditional Segovian cuisine is a reflection of the city's cultural heritage, offering a variety of flavors that are sure to tantalize your taste buds. As you wander through the charming streets of Segovia, you'll find an array of restaurants and taverns serving up local specialties that are steeped in tradition and history. One of the most iconic dishes of Segovian cuisine is the "cochinillo asado" or roasted suckling pig. This delicacy is prepared with great care, following a centuries-old recipe that results in tender, succulent meat with a crispy, golden skin. The cochinillo is typically roasted in a wood-fired oven, which gives it a distinctive flavor that is beloved by locals and visitors alike. Restaurants like Restaurante José María, located at Calle Cronista Lecea, 11, are famous for their cochinillo asado, offering an authentic taste of Segovian culinary tradition.

Another staple of Segovian cuisine is the "judiones de La Granja," large white beans that are grown in the nearby town of La Granja de San Ildefonso. These beans are the star ingredient in a hearty stew, often cooked with chorizo, morcilla (blood sausage), and pork. The dish is a perfect example of the comforting, rustic fare that characterizes Segovian cuisine. For those with a sweet tooth, Segovia offers a range of traditional desserts that are sure to satisfy. One such treat is "ponche segoviano," a layered cake made with sponge cake, cream, and a marzipan coating, then topped with a burnt sugar glaze. This dessert is a favorite in local pastry shops and is a must-try for anyone visiting the city.

To accompany your meal, you might want to try a glass of local wine. The province of Segovia is part of the Vinos de Madrid and Rueda denominations of origin, producing excellent white wines, particularly those made from the Verdejo grape. These wines are a perfect complement to the flavors of Segovian cuisine. In conclusion, traditional Segovian cuisine is an integral part of the city's cultural heritage, offering a culinary journey that is as rich and diverse as its history. From the succulent cochinillo asado to the sweet ponche segoviano, each dish tells a story of tradition and flavor. Exploring the local cuisine is an essential experience for any visitor to Segovia, providing a taste of the city's gastronomic legacy that is sure to leave a lasting impression.

6.2. Cochinillo Asado: Segovia's Signature Dish

Cochinillo asado, or roasted suckling pig, is a culinary treasure that has become synonymous with the city of Segovia. This dish, deeply rooted in tradition, captures the essence of Segovian gastronomy and is a must-try for anyone visiting this historic city. The origins of cochinillo asado in Segovia date back centuries, with the dish being a staple of festive celebrations and family gatherings. The preparation of this delicacy begins with selecting the finest suckling pigs, typically around three weeks old and milk-fed, ensuring the meat is tender and flavorful.

The cooking process is where the magic happens. The pig is seasoned with simple ingredients such as salt, garlic, and sometimes a hint of thyme or bay leaves to enhance the natural flavors. It is then slow-roasted in a wood-fired oven, a method that has been passed down through generations. The high heat and consistent temperature of the oven are crucial, as they ensure the skin of the pig becomes irresistibly crispy while the meat remains succulent and juicy. One of the most iconic places to savor cochinillo asado in Segovia is Restaurante José María. Located in the heart of the city, this renowned restaurant has been serving up this signature dish for decades, earning a reputation for its authenticity and excellence. The cochinillo here is prepared following time-honored techniques, and it's often served with a dramatic flourish, being cut with the edge of a plate to demonstrate its tenderness.

Another notable establishment is Mesón de Cándido, situated at the foot of Segovia's famous aqueduct. This historic restaurant has been a favorite among locals and visitors alike for its traditional ambiance and expertly prepared cochinillo asado. The dining experience at Mesón de Cándido is a journey into Segovia's culinary heritage, with the cochinillo taking center stage. Cochinillo asado is not just a meal; it's an experience that embodies the essence of Segovian cuisine. It's a dish best enjoyed in the company of friends and family, accompanied by a glass of local wine, and savored in the picturesque setting of this ancient city. For anyone visiting Segovia, indulging in this legendary dish is a must, offering a taste of the region's rich gastronomic legacy that is sure to leave a lasting impression.

6.3. Tapas Bars and Local Eateries

In the charming city of Segovia, the tapas bars and local eateries offer a delightful culinary journey, providing a taste of authentic Spanish flavors and the warmth of local hospitality. These establishments are not just places to eat; they are social hubs where friends and families gather to enjoy good food, lively conversation, and the simple pleasures of life. One of the most popular areas for tapas in Segovia is around Plaza Mayor, the city's main square. Here, you'll find a variety of tapas bars and restaurants, each with its own unique atmosphere and specialties. One such place is La Judería, located on Calle de la Infanta Isabel. This cozy eatery is known for its delicious tapas, including local favorites like "tortilla española" (Spanish omelette) and "patatas bravas" (spicy potatoes). The warm, rustic ambiance and friendly service make it a favorite among locals and visitors alike. Another must-visit spot is El Fogón Sefardí, nestled in the heart of Segovia's Jewish Quarter. This restaurant specializes in Sephardic cuisine, offering a unique blend of flavors that reflect the city's rich cultural heritage. Their tapas menu features dishes like "berenjenas a la miel" (honey-glazed eggplant) and "keftas de cordero" (lamb meatballs), providing a delightful gastronomic experience.

For those looking to explore beyond the city center, La Taberna Rubi, located on Calle Gobernador Fernández Jiménez, is a hidden gem. This family-run tavern is known for its warm atmosphere and generous portions. Their "huevos rotos con jamón" (broken eggs with ham) and "croquetas caseras" (homemade croquettes) are particularly popular among patrons. If you're in search of a more modern tapas experience, El Sitio, situated on Calle de los Coches, offers a contemporary twist on traditional Spanish tapas. The chic decor and innovative dishes, such as "tacos de cochinita pibil" (slow-roasted pork tacos) and "tartar de atún" (tuna tartare), make it a trendy spot for a night out. No visit to Segovia would be complete without sampling the local wines and spirits. Many tapas bars in the city offer a selection of regional wines, such as Ribera del Duero and Rueda, as well as local liqueurs like "ponche segoviano" (a sweet, aromatic punch). Pairing these beverages with your tapas enhances the dining experience and provides a true taste of Segovia's culinary landscape.

In conclusion, Segovia's tapas bars and local eateries are an integral part of the city's cultural fabric, offering a window into the local way of life. Whether you're seeking traditional flavors or modern interpretations, these establishments provide a warm welcome and a delicious introduction to the gastronomy of this enchanting Spanish city.

6.4. Gourmet Restaurants and Fine Dining

In the charming city of Segovia, renowned for its historical treasures like the Roman aqueduct and the fairytale-like Alcázar, the culinary scene is equally captivating. Gourmet restaurants and fine dining establishments are scattered throughout the city, offering a delightful experience for food enthusiasts. Here's an exploration of some of the finest dining options in Segovia, where exquisite cuisine meets historic ambiance. One of the most celebrated restaurants in Segovia is Restaurante José María, located in the heart of the city near the Plaza Mayor. This restaurant is famed for its traditional Castilian cuisine, with a particular emphasis on the local specialty, cochinillo asado (roast suckling pig). The elegant dining room, adorned with wooden beams and rustic decor, provides a cozy atmosphere. The extensive wine list, featuring a selection of the finest Spanish wines, complements the dining experience. Another gem in Segovia's culinary landscape is El Sitio, situated in a picturesque spot near the ancient aqueduct. This restaurant offers a blend of traditional and contemporary dishes, with a focus on seasonal ingredients. The modern interior, with its sleek design and ambient lighting, creates a sophisticated dining environment. The outdoor terrace, overlooking the aqueduct, provides a stunning backdrop for a memorable meal. For those seeking a truly luxurious dining experience, the Michelin-starred Restaurante Villena is a must-visit. Located in the Hotel Eurostars Convento Capuchinos, this restaurant boasts an innovative menu crafted by Chef Rubén Arnanz. The dishes are a work of art, combining avant-garde techniques with local flavors. The historic setting of the converted convent adds an extra layer of allure to the dining experience.

La Cocina de Segovia, located near the Alcázar, is another fine dining establishment worth noting. The restaurant is known for its elegant presentation and fusion of traditional Segovian cuisine with modern culinary trends. The dining room, with its classic decor and panoramic views of the city, provides a regal setting for a gourmet meal. For a more intimate dining experience, Restaurante Claustro de San Antonio El Real offers a unique setting within a former monastery. The menu features a selection of refined dishes, with an emphasis on local ingredients and flavors. The tranquil atmosphere of the cloister, combined with the exquisite cuisine, makes for an unforgettable dining experience. In conclusion, Segovia's gourmet restaurants and fine dining establishments offer a diverse array of culinary delights, set against the backdrop of the city's rich history and stunning architecture. Whether you're savoring the traditional flavors of Castilian cuisine or indulging in contemporary culinary creations, Segovia's dining scene is sure to impress even the most discerning food enthusiasts.

6.5. Local Wines and Spirits

In the enchanting city of Segovia, the local wines and spirits are as much a part of the cultural tapestry as its iconic Roman aqueduct and majestic Alcázar. The region surrounding Segovia is blessed with a rich viticultural heritage, producing some of Spain's most esteemed wines. For visitors seeking to immerse themselves in the local flavors, exploring the wines and spirits of Segovia is an essential part of the experience. One of the most prominent wine regions near Segovia is the Ribera del Duero, renowned for its robust red wines made primarily from the Tempranillo grape. Bodegas Protos, located in the town of Peñafiel, is one of the oldest and most esteemed wineries in the region. The winery offers guided tours and tastings, where visitors can explore the vast underground cellars and savor the rich, complex flavors of their wines.

Another notable wine region is the Rueda, situated to the southwest of Segovia. This area is famous for its crisp, aromatic white wines made from the Verdejo grape. Bodegas José Pariente in Rueda is a family-run winery that produces some of the finest Verdejo wines. The modern winery, with its sleek architecture and panoramic views of the vineyards, provides a delightful setting for wine tastings and tours. For those interested in local spirits, the traditional anisette of Segovia is a must-try. This sweet, anise-flavored liqueur has been produced in the region for centuries and is often enjoyed as a digestive after a meal. The most famous brand is Anís de Segovia, which can be found in various bars and shops throughout the city.

In addition to exploring the wineries and distilleries, visitors can experience the local wines and spirits in the numerous bars and restaurants in Segovia. Many establishments offer wine tastings and pairings, allowing guests to sample a selection of regional wines alongside traditional Segovian dishes. For a truly immersive experience, visitors can partake in one of the many wine festivals and events that take place in the region throughout the year. These events offer a unique opportunity to celebrate the local wine culture, meet the winemakers, and enjoy the festive atmosphere.

In conclusion, the local wines and spirits of Segovia are an integral part of the city's charm and heritage. Whether exploring the vineyards and wineries, savoring a glass of Ribera del Duero red or Rueda white in a cozy bar, or toasting with a shot of traditional anisette, the flavors of Segovia are sure to leave a lasting impression on any visitor.

CHAPTER 7

CULTURE AND HERITAGE

7.1. Roman and Medieval Heritage

Segovia, a city steeped in history, is a treasure trove of Roman and medieval heritage. Its ancient streets and monuments tell the stories of a bygone era, making it a fascinating destination for visitors seeking to explore the past. The most iconic symbol of Segovia's Roman heritage is the awe-inspiring Aqueduct. Dating back to the 1st century AD, this engineering marvel stands as a testament to the ingenuity of Roman builders. The aqueduct, with its towering double arches, stretches across the city, providing a majestic backdrop to the old town. Visitors can walk along its base, marveling at the precision of its construction, and climb up to the viewing platform for panoramic views of Segovia.

Another significant Roman site is the remains of the Roman Walls that once encircled the city. Parts of these ancient fortifications can still be seen, offering a glimpse into the defensive strategies of the Roman era. The walls are particularly well-preserved near the Alcázar, where visitors can explore the remnants and learn about the city's strategic importance in Roman times. Segovia's medieval heritage is equally impressive, with the Alcázar being the crown jewel. Perched on a rocky outcrop at the confluence of two rivers, this fairy-tale castle, with its turrets and battlements, seems straight out of a storybook. The Alcázar has a rich history, serving as a royal palace, a military fortress, and even a state prison. Today, it houses a museum where visitors can explore the opulent rooms, admire the medieval artifacts, and enjoy breathtaking views from the Tower of John II. The city's medieval charm is also evident in its old town, a labyrinth of narrow streets and squares lined with historic buildings. The Plaza Mayor, the heart of the city, is surrounded by beautiful medieval and Renaissance structures, including the imposing Segovia Cathedral. This Gothic masterpiece, with its soaring spires and intricate façade, is a must-visit for architecture enthusiasts. Inside, the cathedral's stained glass windows, chapels, and cloisters are a feast for the eyes.

For a deeper dive into Segovia's medieval past, visitors can explore the city's many Romanesque churches, such as the Church of San Millán, the Church of San Esteban, and the Church of San Martín. These churches, with their characteristic round arches and sturdy stone construction, are scattered throughout the city, each with its own unique history and architectural features.

Segovia's Roman and medieval heritage is a captivating blend of architectural grandeur and historical intrigue. From the towering aqueduct to the enchanting Alcázar, and from the ancient Roman walls to the Gothic cathedral, the city offers a journey back in time. Visitors can immerse themselves in the rich history, explore the well-preserved monuments, and experience the medieval charm that makes Segovia a truly remarkable destination.

7.2. Museums and Cultural Institutions

Segovia, a city rich in history and culture, is home to a variety of museums and cultural institutions that offer visitors a deeper understanding of its heritage. These spaces provide a window into the city's past, its artistic achievements, and its vibrant cultural traditions. One of the most prominent museums in Segovia is the Museo de Segovia, located in the historic Casa del Sol. This museum houses an extensive collection of artifacts that span the city's history, from the prehistoric era to the modern day. Visitors can explore exhibits featuring Roman mosaics, medieval sculptures, and fine art from various periods. The museum also offers educational programs and temporary exhibitions, making it a dynamic space for cultural exploration.

Another significant cultural institution is the Museo Zuloaga, situated in the former church of San Juan de los Caballeros. This museum is dedicated to the works of the renowned Spanish painter Ignacio Zuloaga, who lived and worked in Segovia. The collection includes some of his most famous paintings, as well as works by other artists from his personal collection. The museum's setting in a Romanesque church adds to the allure, providing a unique backdrop for the art on display. For those interested in Segovia's religious heritage, the Museo Catedralicio is a must-visit. Located within the

Segovia Cathedral, this museum showcases a rich collection of religious art, including paintings, sculptures, and liturgical objects. Highlights include the Flemish tapestries and the exquisite choir books. The museum also offers breathtaking views of the cathedral's interior, including its magnificent stained glass windows.

The Real Casa de Moneda, or Royal Mint, is another cultural highlight in Segovia. This museum is housed in a historic building that was once the royal mint of Spain. Visitors can learn about the history of coin production and see the original minting machinery. The museum also hosts temporary exhibitions on various themes related to Segovia's economic and industrial history. For a contemporary cultural experience, the Centro de Interpretación del Barrio de San Lorenzo y Los Valles offers insights into the traditional neighborhoods of Segovia. This center provides an interactive journey through the city's urban development, local customs, and community life. It's an excellent way to understand the social fabric of Segovia and its evolution over time.

In conclusion, Segovia's museums and cultural institutions are essential destinations for anyone seeking to immerse themselves in the city's rich history and artistic heritage. From ancient artifacts to contemporary exhibitions, these spaces offer a diverse range of experiences that provide a deeper appreciation of Segovia's cultural legacy.

7.3. Religious Architecture and Monasteries

Segovia, a city steeped in history, is renowned for its impressive religious architecture and monasteries that dot its landscape. These sacred structures are not only places of worship but also serve as a testament to the city's rich cultural and historical heritage. The Segovia Cathedral, also known as the Cathedral of Saint Mary, is one of the city's most iconic landmarks. Located in the main square, Plaza Mayor, this magnificent Gothic structure is often referred to as the "Lady of Cathedrals" due to its elegance and grandeur. The cathedral's towering spires, intricate façade, and stunning stained glass windows make it a must-visit for anyone interested in religious architecture. Inside, visitors can explore its numerous chapels, the cloister, and the museum, which houses a collection of religious art and artifacts.

Another significant religious site in Segovia is the Monastery of San Antonio El Real. This monastery is known for its unique Mudéjar architecture, characterized by intricate stucco work and ornamental tilework. The highlight of the monastery is the cloister, with its beautifully decorated ceiling and walls. The monastery also features a museum that displays religious art and artifacts, providing visitors with a glimpse into its rich history. The Church of San Millán is another architectural gem in Segovia. Dating back to the 12th century, this Romanesque church is one of the oldest in the city. Its striking façade, adorned with a rose window and carved stone figures, is a fine example of Romanesque art. The interior of the church is equally impressive, with its three naves and a collection of ancient frescoes.

For those interested in exploring monastic life, the Monastery of Santa María del Parral is a serene retreat. Located on the outskirts of the city, this monastery is surrounded by lush gardens and offers a peaceful atmosphere. The monastery's church is a beautiful example of late Gothic architecture, and visitors can also explore the cloister and the refectory, which are adorned with frescoes and religious artworks. The Church of San Esteban is another notable religious site in Segovia. This church is known for its impressive Romanesque tower, which is one of the tallest in the city. The interior of the church features a beautiful altarpiece and a collection of religious sculptures and paintings.

In conclusion, Segovia's religious architecture and monasteries are a testament to the city's rich cultural and spiritual heritage. From the grandeur of the Segovia Cathedral to the serene beauty of the Monastery of Santa María del Parral, these sacred sites offer visitors a chance to explore the city's history and architectural prowess. Whether you are interested in religious art, architecture, or simply seeking a peaceful retreat, Segovia's religious landmarks are sure to leave a lasting impression.

7.4. Traditional Festivals and Events

Segovia, a city rich in history and culture, comes alive with a variety of traditional festivals and events throughout the year. These celebrations offer visitors a unique opportunity to immerse themselves in the local customs, enjoy vibrant performances, and savor the flavors of regional cuisine. One of the most anticipated events in Segovia is the Festival of San Juan and San Pedro, held in late June. This festival marks the beginning of summer and is celebrated with a series of concerts, dance performances, and outdoor activities. The streets of Segovia are adorned with colorful decorations, and the air is filled with the sounds of music and laughter. The highlight of the festival is the procession of the giants and bigheads, a traditional parade featuring large papier-mâché figures that dance through the city's historic center.

Another significant event is the Titirimundi International Puppet Festival, which takes place in May. This festival attracts puppeteers and performers from all over the world, transforming Segovia into a magical world of puppetry and storytelling. The performances range from traditional puppet shows to innovative and contemporary acts, catering to audiences of all ages. The festival's atmosphere is enchanting, with puppet shows held in various venues, including the city's squares, theaters, and even the iconic Alcázar. Segovia also celebrates its rich culinary heritage with the Fiesta de la Matanza, a traditional pig slaughter festival held in February. This event showcases the age-old practice of preparing and preserving pork products for the winter months. Visitors can witness the various stages of the process, from the butchering of the pig to the making of chorizos and other delicacies. The festival is a gastronomic delight, with tastings of local dishes and a festive market selling artisanal products.

The Holy Week in Segovia is another important religious event, marked by solemn processions and ceremonies. The city's streets are filled with the sound of marching bands and the sight of hooded penitents carrying religious statues. The processions are a moving display of faith and tradition, with the most impressive one taking place on Good Friday, when the statues of the Virgin Mary and Jesus are paraded through the city in a candlelit procession. In conclusion, Segovia's traditional festivals and events are a vibrant expression of the city's cultural heritage. From the lively celebrations of San Juan and San Pedro to the enchanting puppetry of Titirimundi, and from the gastronomic delights of the Fiesta de la Matanza to the solemnity of Holy Week, these festivities offer visitors a chance to experience the rich tapestry of Segovian life. Whether you are interested in music, theater, food, or religious traditions, Segovia's festivals and events provide a window into the heart and soul of this historic city.

7.5. Arts and Crafts of Segovia

Segovia, a city steeped in history and culture, is also a vibrant center for arts and crafts. The city's artisans and craftsmen preserve traditional techniques while also embracing contemporary styles, creating a unique blend of old and new. For visitors interested in exploring the local arts and crafts scene, Segovia offers a wealth of opportunities to discover handmade treasures and artistic expressions. One of the most iconic crafts of Segovia is the traditional pottery, known for its intricate designs and vibrant colors. The Barrio de los Potters, or the Potters' Quarter, is a must-visit area where you can find workshops and studios dedicated to this ancient craft. Here, artisans like Alfarería San Juan de los Caballeros and Cerámica Nieva showcase their skills, creating beautiful ceramics ranging from decorative tiles to functional tableware. Visitors can watch the potters at work, learn about the techniques used, and even purchase unique pieces to take home.

Textile arts are also a significant part of Segovia's cultural heritage. The city is known for its woolen products, thanks to its historical connection to the wool trade. Shops like Lana Serena offer a modern take on traditional woolen crafts, producing high-quality garments and accessories made from locally sourced wool. The attention to detail and the use of natural materials make these textiles a popular choice for those seeking sustainable and stylish fashion. Leatherwork is another craft that has a long history in Segovia. Artisans like Marroquinería La Muralla specialize in creating leather goods such as bags, belts, and wallets, using time-honored techniques. The craftsmanship is evident in the intricate designs and the durability of the products, making them a favorite among locals and visitors alike.

For those interested in decorative arts, Segovia is home to several workshops and galleries where you can find a variety of handcrafted items. From intricate metalwork to delicate glassware, the city's artists and craftsmen produce a wide range of decorative pieces that reflect the region's artistic traditions. Galleries like Sala Ex.Presa 2 and La Alhóndiga often showcase the works of local artists, providing a platform for them to display their talent and creativity. In conclusion, the arts and crafts of Segovia are a testament to the city's rich cultural heritage and the creativity of its artisans. Whether you're drawn to traditional pottery, exquisite textiles, fine leatherwork, or decorative arts, Segovia offers a treasure trove of handmade wonders. Exploring the workshops, studios, and galleries of this historic city is a journey into the heart of its artistic soul, where the past and present merge in beautiful and unexpected ways.

CHAPTER 8

OUTDOOR ACTIVITIES AND ADVENTURES

8.1. Hiking and Nature Trails

Segovia, a city renowned for its historical and architectural wonders, is also a gateway to some of the most beautiful natural landscapes in the region. The surrounding countryside offers a variety of hiking and nature trails that allow visitors to explore the scenic beauty and diverse ecosystems of the area. One of the most popular hiking destinations near Segovia is the Natural Park of the Sierra de Guadarrama. This mountain range, located just a short drive from the city, is a haven for outdoor enthusiasts, with its rugged peaks, lush forests, and crystal-clear streams. The park offers a network of well-marked trails suitable for all levels of hikers. One of the most scenic routes is the hike to the peak of Peñalara, the highest point in the Sierra de Guadarrama. The trail takes you through pine forests and alpine meadows, with breathtaking views of the surrounding mountains and valleys.

Another great destination for nature lovers is the Duratón River Gorges Natural Park. This park is famous for its dramatic limestone cliffs that rise above the meandering Duratón River. The park has several hiking trails that wind along the riverbanks and through the gorges, offering stunning views of the cliffs and the opportunity to spot a variety of bird species, including the majestic griffon vulture. The Ermita de San Frutos trail is a popular choice, leading to an ancient hermitage perched on a rocky outcrop overlooking the river. For those interested in exploring the local flora and fauna, the Eresma River Valley offers a gentle hike through a picturesque landscape. The trail follows the course of the Eresma River, passing through meadows, woodlands, and traditional farmlands. Along the way, hikers can enjoy the sights and sounds of nature, including the diverse birdlife and the soothing sound of the flowing river.

The Royal Palace of La Granja de San Ildefonso, located just outside Segovia, is surrounded by beautiful gardens and forested areas that are perfect for leisurely walks.

The trails around the palace lead through formal gardens, past fountains and sculptures, and into the tranquil woods. The peaceful ambiance and the stunning baroque architecture of the palace make this an ideal spot for a relaxing stroll. In conclusion, the hiking and nature trails around Segovia offer a wonderful opportunity to experience the natural beauty of the region. Whether you're looking for a challenging mountain hike, a leisurely walk along a river, or a peaceful stroll through historic gardens, the area around Segovia has something to suit every preference. These trails provide a perfect escape into nature, where visitors can unwind, enjoy the fresh air, and discover the scenic landscapes that lie just beyond the city's historic walls.

8.2. Cycling Routes and Bike Rentals

Segovia, with its picturesque landscapes and historic charm, is an ideal destination for cycling enthusiasts. The city and its surrounding areas offer a variety of cycling routes that cater to all levels of experience, from leisurely rides through the countryside to more challenging routes that explore the rugged terrain of the nearby mountains. One of the most popular cycling routes in Segovia is the Greenway (Vía Verde) of the Eresma River. This gentle, family-friendly route follows the course of the river and is perfect for a leisurely ride. The path is well-marked and takes cyclists through beautiful natural scenery, past historic mills, and offers stunning views of the Alcázar and the city's Roman aqueduct. The Greenway is also suitable for walkers and runners, making it a versatile option for outdoor enthusiasts.

For those seeking a more adventurous ride, the cycling routes in the Sierra de Guadarrama National Park provide a thrilling experience. The park's diverse landscape includes mountainous terrain, dense forests, and alpine meadows, offering challenging climbs and exhilarating descents. One of the popular routes is the climb to Puerto de Navacerrada, a mountain pass that offers breathtaking views of the surrounding peaks and valleys. Segovia's countryside is crisscrossed with quiet country roads that are perfect for cycling. These routes offer a chance to explore the region's charming villages, vineyards, and historic sites at a leisurely pace. The ride from Segovia to the Royal Palace of La Granja de San Ildefonso is a particularly scenic route, with the stunning backdrop of the Sierra de Guadarrama and the beautiful gardens of the palace awaiting at the end. For those who do not have their own bikes, there are several bike rental shops in Segovia that offer a range of bicycles for hire, including mountain bikes, road bikes, and electric bikes. BiciSegovia is one of the well-known rental shops in the city, located conveniently near the city center. They provide not only bike rentals but also helmets, locks, and maps to ensure a safe and enjoyable cycling experience. Another option is Alquiler de Bicicletas Segovia, which offers guided cycling tours in addition to bike rentals, allowing visitors to explore the area with the expertise of a local guide.

In conclusion, cycling in Segovia offers a unique way to experience the natural beauty and historic sites of the region. Whether you prefer a leisurely ride along the river, a challenging mountain adventure, or a scenic tour of the countryside, there are plenty of cycling routes to suit your preferences. With the convenience of bike rental services, exploring Segovia on two wheels has never been easier, making it a must-do activity for any visitor to this enchanting city.

8.3. Bird Watching and Wildlife Observation

Segovia, a city renowned for its architectural splendor, is also a haven for nature enthusiasts, offering a wealth of opportunities for bird watching and wildlife observation. The diverse landscapes surrounding the city, from rolling hills to river valleys, provide habitats for a variety of bird species and other wildlife, making it a perfect destination for those looking to connect with nature. One of the prime locations for bird watching in Segovia is the Natural Park of the Sierra de Guadarrama. This mountainous area is home to a wide range of bird species, including the majestic Spanish imperial eagle, the Eurasian black vulture, and the colorful European bee-eater. The park's varied ecosystems, from alpine meadows to dense forests, offer excellent opportunities for spotting these and many other species in their natural habitats. The visitor center at Boca del Asno provides information on the best trails and observation points within the park.

Another important birding site is the Duratón River Gorges Natural Park, located northeast of Segovia. The park is famous for its large colonies of griffon vultures, which can be seen soaring above the dramatic limestone cliffs. In addition to vultures, the park is also a habitat for other raptors, such as peregrine falcons and golden eagles. The park offers guided bird-watching tours, where visitors can learn more about the local avian fauna and the best spots for observation. The Eresma River Valley, close to Segovia, is another excellent area for bird watching. The riverbanks and surrounding wetlands attract a variety of waterfowl, including herons, egrets, and ducks. The area is also a stopping point for migratory birds, making it a dynamic spot for bird watching throughout the year.

For those interested in a more leisurely bird-watching experience, the Royal Palace of La Granja de San Ildefonso, with its extensive gardens and woodlands, provides a tranquil setting for observing garden and forest birds. The palace grounds are home to species such as the European robin, the great tit, and the Eurasian wren. In conclusion, Segovia and its surrounding areas offer a rich tapestry of habitats for bird watching and wildlife observation. Whether you're an experienced birder or a casual observer, the region's natural parks, river valleys, and historic gardens provide ample opportunities to encounter the diverse birdlife and wildlife of this beautiful part of Spain.

8.4. Adventure Sports: Hot Air Ballooning and Paragliding

Segovia, a city known for its rich history and stunning architecture, also offers thrilling experiences for adventure seekers. Among the most popular adventure sports in the area are hot air ballooning and paragliding, providing unique perspectives of the city's iconic landmarks and the surrounding landscape. Hot air ballooning in Segovia is an unforgettable experience, offering breathtaking views of the city's famous aqueduct, the Alcázar, and the Cathedral from above. Several companies, such as Globos Boreal and Siempre en las Nubes, operate balloon flights that take off at dawn, providing passengers with a serene and picturesque journey over the city and the countryside. The flights typically last about an hour, and many companies offer a celebratory toast with cava and a flight certificate upon landing. Some even provide transportation back to the launch site, making the experience hassle-free for visitors.

Paragliding is another popular adventure sport in the Segovia region, particularly in the nearby Sierra de Guadarrama mountains. The area's favorable wind conditions and scenic landscapes make it an ideal spot for both beginners and experienced paragliders. Companies like Parapente Segovia and Parapente Factory offer tandem flights, where participants are accompanied by a professional instructor. These flights allow visitors to soar over the mountains and valleys, experiencing the thrill of free flight. For those looking to learn the sport, these companies also offer courses ranging from introductory sessions to advanced training. Both hot air ballooning and paragliding in Segovia provide not only an adrenaline rush but also a unique way to appreciate the beauty of the region. Whether floating gently in a balloon or gliding through the air with a paraglider, participants are treated to unparalleled views of the historic city and its natural surroundings. It's an experience that combines adventure with awe, leaving visitors with lasting memories of their time in Segovia.

In conclusion, for those looking to add a touch of adventure to their visit to Segovia, hot air ballooning and paragliding are must-try activities. These sports offer a different perspective of the city and its landscapes, providing both excitement and breathtaking vistas. With experienced operators ensuring safety and comfort, visitors can enjoy these thrilling experiences with peace of mind.

8.5. Golf Courses and Outdoor Recreation

Segovia, a city renowned for its historical and cultural heritage, also offers a range of outdoor recreational activities, including golf, that cater to visitors looking for a more active and leisurely experience. The region's natural beauty, with its rolling hills, lush forests, and scenic vistas, provides an idyllic backdrop for golf enthusiasts and outdoor adventurers alike. One of the notable golf courses in the Segovia area is the Club de Golf La Faisanera. Located just a short drive from the city, this 18-hole course is set amidst the picturesque landscape of the Sierra de Guadarrama mountains. The course is known for its challenging layout, with undulating fairways, strategically placed bunkers, and water hazards that test the skills of golfers of all levels. La Faisanera also boasts excellent facilities, including a driving range, putting green, and a clubhouse with a restaurant and pro shop. The stunning views of the mountains and the serene environment make it a popular choice for both local and visiting golfers.

For those seeking a more casual golfing experience, the Pitch & Putt de Segovia offers a shorter, 9-hole course that is perfect for beginners or for a quick round of golf. The course is located near the city center, making it easily accessible for visitors. The facility also provides equipment rental, making it convenient for travelers who may not have their golf gear with them. Apart from golf, Segovia and its surroundings offer a plethora of outdoor activities. Hiking and cycling are popular, with numerous trails winding through the countryside and the nearby Sierra de Guadarrama National Park. For water enthusiasts, the Duratón River and the reservoirs of the region, such as the Embalse del Pontón Alto, provide opportunities for kayaking, fishing, and even swimming in designated areas.

Horseback riding is another activity that visitors can enjoy, with several equestrian centers offering guided rides through the scenic landscapes around Segovia. These rides offer a unique way to explore the countryside and connect with nature. In conclusion, Segovia is not only a city of historical and architectural marvels but also a destination for outdoor recreation and golf enthusiasts. The Club de Golf La Faisanera and the Pitch & Putt de Segovia cater to golfers of all levels, while the natural beauty of the region offers a wide range of activities for those looking to enjoy the great outdoors. Whether it's teeing off against a backdrop of mountains, paddling down a tranquil river, or exploring the countryside on horseback, Segovia provides a perfect blend of leisure, adventure, and scenic beauty.

8.6 Family and Kids Friendly Activities

Segovia, with its enchanting castle, ancient aqueduct, and charming old town, is a delightful destination for families traveling with children. The city offers a range of activities that are both educational and entertaining, ensuring that visitors of all ages have a memorable experience. One of the top family-friendly attractions in Segovia is the Alcázar of Segovia. This fairy-tale castle, said to have inspired Walt Disney's Cinderella Castle, is a must-visit for families. Children will be fascinated by the castle's towers, drawbridge, and moat. Inside, the armory room, with its collection of medieval weapons and armor, is particularly popular with young visitors. The castle also offers breathtaking views of the surrounding countryside from its towers.

The Aqueduct of Segovia is another iconic landmark that impresses visitors of all ages. This ancient Roman engineering marvel, with its towering arches, provides a great opportunity for families to learn about history and architecture. The area around the aqueduct is pedestrian-friendly, making it safe for children to explore. For a fun and educational experience, the Centro Didáctico de la Judería offers interactive exhibits about the history of Segovia's Jewish community. The center is located in the old Jewish quarter, and its activities are designed to engage children while they learn about the city's cultural heritage. The Casa de los Picos is another interesting stop for families. This historic building, known for its façade adorned with over 600 granite spikes, houses the Segovia Art School and an exhibition hall. The exhibitions often include works that are appealing to children, such as colorful paintings and sculptures.

Outdoor activities are plentiful in Segovia, with numerous parks and green spaces where families can enjoy picnics and leisurely walks. The Jardines del Alcázar, located below the castle, offer a peaceful setting with beautiful gardens and stunning views of the city. The Parque de la Dehesa, the largest park in Segovia, features playgrounds, sports facilities, and plenty of open space for children to run and play. For a unique adventure, families can take a hot air balloon ride over Segovia. Companies like Siempre en las Nubes offer balloon flights that provide a bird's-eye view of the city's landmarks, including the aqueduct, the Alcázar, and the cathedral. This unforgettable experience is sure to be a highlight of any family trip to Segovia.

In conclusion, Segovia is a family-friendly destination that offers a mix of historical, cultural, and outdoor activities. From exploring the grandeur of the Alcázar to strolling through the city's parks, there is something for every member of the family to enjoy. With its safe and welcoming atmosphere, Segovia is an ideal place for families to create lasting memories together.

8.7 Activities for Solo Travelers

Segovia, a city rich in history and culture, is a wonderful destination for solo travelers seeking adventure, relaxation, and self-discovery. The city offers a variety of activities that cater to different interests, ensuring that solo visitors have a fulfilling and memorable experience. One of the must-do activities for solo travelers in Segovia is exploring the iconic Aqueduct of Segovia. This ancient Roman engineering marvel is not only a symbol of the city but also a testament to its historical significance. Solo travelers can take their time admiring the structure, capturing photographs, and learning about its history through informative plaques and guided tours.

A visit to the Alcázar of Segovia is another activity that solo travelers will find rewarding. This fairy-tale castle, perched on a rocky outcrop, offers breathtaking views of the surrounding landscape. Inside, visitors can explore the beautifully decorated rooms, climb the Tower of Juan II for panoramic views, and delve into the castle's rich history. For those interested in art and culture, the Museo de Arte Contemporáneo Esteban Vicente is a must-visit. This museum, dedicated to the works of the Spanish abstract artist Esteban Vicente, is housed in a beautifully restored palace. Solo travelers can enjoy the tranquil atmosphere as they wander through the galleries, admiring the vibrant artworks and learning about the artist's life and legacy.

Solo travelers seeking a peaceful retreat can spend time at the Jardines del Alcázar. These gardens, located below the Alcázar, offer a serene escape from the city's hustle and bustle. Visitors can stroll along the pathways, relax by the fountains, and enjoy the stunning views of the city and countryside. For a unique experience, solo travelers can embark on a hot air balloon ride over Segovia. Companies like Siempre en las Nubes offer flights that provide a bird's-eye view of the city's landmarks, including the aqueduct, the Alcázar, and the cathedral. This unforgettable experience is a perfect way for solo travelers to see the city from a different perspective.

Exploring the old Jewish quarter is another activity that solo travelers will find enriching. This historic area, with its narrow streets and charming buildings, offers a glimpse into Segovia's multicultural past. Visitors can learn about the history of the Jewish community in Segovia at the Centro Didáctico de la Judería and visit the ancient synagogue, now the Convent of Corpus Christi. For those interested in local cuisine, a visit to the Mercado de la Plaza Mayor is a must. This traditional market offers a variety of local products, including cheeses, meats, and pastries. Solo travelers can sample different delicacies, chat with the vendors, and even pick up some ingredients for a picnic in one of the city's parks.

Lastly, solo travelers can join a guided walking tour of Segovia. These tours, offered by various companies, provide an in-depth look at the city's history, architecture, and culture. It's also a great opportunity for solo travelers to meet other visitors and share their experiences. In conclusion, Segovia offers a wide range of activities for solo travelers, from exploring historic landmarks and enjoying art and culture to experiencing unique adventures and savoring local cuisine. With its welcoming atmosphere and diverse attractions, Segovia is an ideal destination for those traveling alone.

CHAPTER 9

SHOPPING IN SEGOVIA

Click on the Link or Scan the QR Code with a device to view a comprehensive map of Shopping Districts in Segovia – https://shorturl.at/uyJW3

9.1. Traditional Markets and Local Products

Segovia, a city renowned for its historical charm and gastronomic delights, offers a variety of traditional markets that provide a window into the local culture and cuisine. These markets are not only places to shop but also vibrant spaces where locals and visitors alike can immerse themselves in the authentic Segovian lifestyle. This essay explores six traditional markets in Segovia, highlighting their offerings, locations, and the local products that make them unique.

Mercado de la Plaza Mayor: The Heart of Segovia

The Mercado de la Plaza Mayor is situated in the bustling main square of Segovia, surrounded by historic buildings and lively cafes. This market is known for its fresh produce, including fruits, vegetables, and herbs, sourced from the surrounding countryside. Visitors can also find a selection of local cheeses, such as the famous Queso de Oveja, and cured meats, including the renowned Chorizo de Cantimpalos. Prices are reasonable, making it an ideal spot for picking up ingredients for a picnic or a home-cooked meal.

Mercado de San Millán: A Gourmet Experience

Located in the San Millán neighborhood, the Mercado de San Millán is a smaller, more specialized market that offers a variety of gourmet products. Here, food enthusiasts can discover artisanal bread, handcrafted chocolates, and a selection of wines from the

Ribera del Duero region. The market is also a great place to sample and purchase the local delicacy, Cochinillo Asado (roast suckling pig), with prices varying depending on the vendor and the quality of the product.

Mercado de la Albuera: A Local Favorite

The Mercado de la Albuera, set in the historic Albuera district, is a favorite among locals for its fresh seafood and meat. The market boasts a variety of fish stalls, offering everything from trout, a regional specialty, to seafood caught off the Spanish coast. Meat lovers can find high-quality cuts of beef, lamb, and pork, perfect for grilling or roasting. Prices are competitive, making it a popular choice for everyday shopping.

Mercado Ecológico: Embracing Sustainability

The Mercado Ecológico, held monthly in the Plaza de San Lorenzo, is dedicated to organic and sustainable products. This market features stalls selling organic fruits and vegetables, eco-friendly household items, and natural cosmetics. Visitors can also find a range of gluten-free and vegan products, catering to various dietary needs. Prices are slightly higher due to the organic certification, but the quality and environmental benefits are worth the extra cost.

Feria de Artesanía: A Celebration of Craftsmanship

The Feria de Artesanía, held annually in the Plaza Mayor, is a showcase of local craftsmanship and artisanal products. This market is an excellent place to find unique souvenirs, including hand-painted ceramics, woven textiles, and traditional jewelry. Visitors can also enjoy live demonstrations of crafts such as pottery making and wood carving. Prices vary depending on the item, but bargaining is common, so don't be afraid to negotiate.

Mercadillo de Segovia: A Weekly Affair

The Mercadillo de Segovia, held every Thursday in the Plaza de la Universidad, is a weekly flea market where visitors can find a wide range of goods, from clothing and accessories to household items and antiques. While not specifically focused on food, the market does offer some local products, such as honey, jams, and pastries. It's a great place to browse and discover hidden treasures at affordable prices.

Segovia's traditional markets are a testament to the city's rich culinary heritage and its commitment to fresh, local produce. Each market offers a unique experience, allowing visitors to explore the flavors of the region, from farm-fresh ingredients to artisanal delights. Whether you're a food lover, a bargain hunter, or simply in search of an authentic local experience, Segovia's markets provide a delightful journey through the tastes and textures of this historic city.

9.2. Artisanal Shops and Handcrafted Goods

Segovia, a city rich in history and tradition, is also a haven for those seeking authentic artisanal shops and handcrafted goods. The narrow streets and charming squares of the old town are dotted with small boutiques and workshops, where skilled artisans keep age-old crafts alive. One of the most notable artisanal shops in Segovia is Cerámica Duque. Located near the iconic Aqueduct, this family-run workshop has been producing traditional Segovian ceramics for generations. Visitors can find a wide range of hand-painted pottery, including plates, bowls, and decorative tiles, each piece showcasing the intricate designs and vibrant colors characteristic of the region's ceramic art. The shop also offers demonstrations, allowing visitors to see the artisans at work and learn about the techniques used in creating these beautiful pieces.

Another must-visit destination for handcrafted goods is La Casa del Arcipestre, situated in the picturesque Plaza de Medina del Campo. This shop specializes in hand-woven textiles, offering a selection of scarves, shawls, and table linens made from natural fibers such as wool, silk, and linen. The intricate patterns and delicate craftsmanship of these textiles reflect the rich textile tradition of Segovia. For those interested in leather goods, Marroquinería La Muralla is a treasure trove of handcrafted items. Located near the city walls, this workshop produces a variety of leather products, including bags, belts, and wallets. Each piece is made with care and attention to detail, ensuring both quality and durability. The shop also offers personalized services, allowing visitors to have items custom-made to their specifications.

Segovia is also known for its traditional confectionery, and a visit to La Confitería El Alcázar is a sweet treat for any visitor. This historic shop, located close to the Alcázar, has been delighting locals and tourists alike with its handmade sweets and pastries for over a century. Their specialty, the ponche segoviano, is a must-try, but they also offer a variety of other treats, including marzipan, chocolates, and candied fruits.

In conclusion, Segovia's artisanal shops and handcrafted goods offer a glimpse into the city's rich cultural heritage and provide visitors with a unique shopping experience. From traditional ceramics and textiles to leather goods and sweets, these shops showcase the skill and creativity of Segovian artisans. Whether you're looking for a special souvenir or a piece of authentic Spanish craftsmanship, Segovia's artisanal shops are sure to have something to catch your eye.

9.3. Fashion Boutiques and Designer Stores

Segovia, a city known for its rich history and cultural heritage, also boasts a selection of fashion boutiques and designer stores that cater to the style-conscious traveler. These shops offer a mix of traditional and contemporary fashion, showcasing the creativity and craftsmanship of local and international designers. One of the standout fashion boutiques in Segovia is Moda Vandi, located in the heart of the city near Plaza Mayor. This chic boutique offers a carefully curated selection of women's clothing and accessories from both established and emerging designers. The store's elegant interior provides a welcoming atmosphere for shoppers, and the friendly staff are always on hand to offer personalized styling advice.

Another must-visit boutique is Almudena Navalón, situated on Calle Real, one of Segovia's main shopping streets. This store specializes in high-end fashion, featuring a range of designer labels that are perfect for special occasions or adding a touch of luxury to your everyday wardrobe. The boutique's sophisticated decor and attentive service make for a delightful shopping experience. For those interested in contemporary Spanish fashion, La Mona Checa is a trendy boutique that showcases the latest collections from up-and-coming Spanish designers. Located on Calle Juan Bravo, this store is a favorite among fashion-forward locals and visitors alike. The boutique's modern aesthetic and eclectic selection of clothing and accessories make it a great place to discover new trends and unique pieces. Segovia is also home to several multi-brand stores that offer a diverse selection of fashion and accessories. Tienda Travesía, located on Calle de la Trinidad, is a popular destination for those looking to explore a variety of styles and brands under one roof. The store features a mix of casual and formal wear, as well as a selection of shoes, bags, and jewelry.

In conclusion, Segovia's fashion boutiques and designer stores provide a delightful shopping experience for those looking to add some Spanish flair to their wardrobe. From elegant designer boutiques to trendy multi-brand stores, the city offers a range of options to suit different tastes and budgets. Whether you're searching for a special outfit or simply browsing the latest trends, Segovia's fashion scene is sure to impress.

9.4. Souvenirs and Specialty Items

Segovia, a city steeped in history and culture, offers visitors a wide range of souvenirs and specialty items that capture the essence of this enchanting destination. From traditional crafts to gastronomic delights, there are plenty of unique keepsakes to take home as a reminder of your time in Segovia. One of the most iconic souvenirs from Segovia is the miniature replica of the Roman Aqueduct. These replicas come in various sizes and materials, including stone, wood, and metal, making them a perfect memento of the city's architectural marvel. You can find these at souvenir shops scattered around the Plaza del Azoguejo and along Calle Real. Ceramics and pottery are also popular souvenirs in Segovia, reflecting the region's rich artisanal heritage. Cerámica Duque, located near the Aqueduct, is a family-run workshop where you can find hand-painted ceramics featuring traditional Segovian designs. From decorative plates and tiles to functional kitchenware, these pieces are a beautiful addition to any home.

For those with a sweet tooth, Segovia's famous dessert, Ponche Segoviano, is a must-buy. This layered cake, made with marzipan and custard cream, is a local delicacy. Confitería El Alcázar, a historic confectionery near the Alcázar, is renowned for its authentic Ponche Segoviano, which they can package for travel. Segovia is also known for its high-quality textiles, particularly woolen goods. La Lana de Segovia is a store specializing in wool products, including scarves, shawls, and blankets, made from the wool of local sheep. These cozy items are not only practical but also serve as a warm reminder of your visit to Segovia.

Leather goods are another specialty of the region. Marroquinería La Muralla offers a wide range of handcrafted leather items, from bags and wallets to belts and accessories. The craftsmanship and quality of these products make them a lasting and stylish souvenir. For something truly unique, consider purchasing a piece of Segovian goldwork embroidery. This intricate craft is a traditional art form in Segovia, and you can find exquisite examples of goldwork on items like purses, fans, and even framed artwork at specialty shops in the old town.

In conclusion, Segovia offers a diverse array of souvenirs and specialty items that reflect the city's rich history, culture, and craftsmanship. Whether you're looking for a traditional keepsake, a tasty treat, or a piece of artisanal art, you're sure to find the perfect memento for your visit to this captivating city.

9.5. Modern Shopping Centers and Outlets

While Segovia is renowned for its historic charm and traditional artisanal shops, the city also offers modern shopping experiences for those seeking contemporary retail options. Several shopping centers and outlets in and around Segovia provide a wide range of products, from international brands to local specialties, catering to the needs and preferences of visitors and locals alike. One of the most popular modern shopping destinations in Segovia is the Luz de Castilla Shopping Center. Located on the outskirts of the city, this large shopping mall offers a diverse selection of stores, including fashion boutiques, electronics shops, and home decor outlets. The center also features a supermarket, a cinema complex, and a food court with various dining options. Luz de Castilla provides ample parking and is easily accessible by public transport, making it a convenient option for a day of shopping.

For those looking for designer brands at discounted prices, the Las Rozas Village outlet mall is a short drive from Segovia. This chic outdoor shopping village is home to over 100 boutiques offering up to 60% off on luxury and high-street brands. The picturesque setting, with its tree-lined streets and elegant storefronts, creates a pleasant shopping atmosphere. In addition to fashion, visitors can find accessories, cosmetics, and homeware. The village also has several cafes and restaurants for a relaxing break between shopping. In the heart of Segovia, the Plaza Mayor and surrounding streets offer a more contemporary shopping experience amidst the city's historic architecture. Here, visitors can find a mix of modern boutiques and international chain stores, selling clothing, accessories, and gadgets. The area is also home to several bookstores, gift shops, and specialty food stores, providing a varied shopping experience. For a unique shopping experience, the Mercado de la Albuera is a modern market located in the city center. This indoor market features a variety of stalls selling fresh produce, gourmet products, and artisanal goods. The market is a great place to explore the local culinary scene and pick up some fresh ingredients or ready-to-eat snacks.

In conclusion, Segovia offers a blend of traditional and modern shopping experiences. From the expansive Luz de Castilla Shopping Center to the chic boutiques of Las Rozas Village and the contemporary offerings in the city center, visitors have a wide range of options to satisfy their shopping needs. Whether you're looking for the latest fashion trends, electronic gadgets, or local delicacies, Segovia's shopping centers and outlets provide a convenient and enjoyable retail experience.

CHAPTER 10

DAY TRIPS AND EXCURSIONS

10.1. Avila: City of Saints and Stones

Ávila, often referred to as the "City of Saints and Stones," is a historic gem located near Segovia in the Castile and León region of Spain. Renowned for its well-preserved medieval walls and its deep religious heritage, Ávila offers visitors a unique journey through time, where ancient stones tell tales of faith and fortitude. The most iconic feature of Ávila is its imposing city walls, which date back to the 11th and 12th centuries. These walls, which stretch for about 2.5 kilometers, encircle the old town and are punctuated by 88 towers and nine gates. Visitors can walk along the top of the walls, an activity that provides breathtaking views of the city and the surrounding countryside. The Puerta del Alcázar, the main gate, is a particularly impressive entry point, leading directly into the heart of the old town.

Within the walls, the Cathedral of Ávila stands as a testament to the city's religious significance. This cathedral, which is considered the first Gothic cathedral in Spain, also serves as a fortress, with its apse forming part of the city's defensive walls. The interior of the cathedral is a treasure trove of religious art, including a beautiful altarpiece, stunning stained glass windows, and the tomb of El Tostado, a notable Spanish bishop and scholar. Ávila is also famous for being the birthplace of Saint Teresa of Ávila, a Carmelite nun and mystic who founded the Discalced Carmelite Order. The Convent of Saint Teresa, built on the site of her birthplace, is a key pilgrimage site. Visitors can explore the chapel, which houses relics of the saint, and the small museum that provides insights into her life and work.

Another important religious site is the Monastery of Saint Thomas, which houses the Museum of Oriental Art and the Museum of Natural Sciences. The monastery's church is a magnificent example of Gothic architecture, and the cloisters are a peaceful retreat from the bustling city. For those interested in the city's history and culture, the Ávila

Provincial Museum, located in the Renaissance-style Palacio de los Serrano, offers a fascinating collection of artifacts, including Roman mosaics, medieval sculptures, and traditional costumes.

In conclusion, Ávila, the "City of Saints and Stones," is a captivating destination that offers a rich tapestry of history, religion, and architecture. From its impressive city walls and Gothic cathedral to its deep connections with Saint Teresa of Ávila, the city provides a unique and memorable experience for visitors. Whether exploring the ancient streets, visiting the sacred sites, or simply enjoying the views from the walls, Ávila is a place where the past is palpably present in every stone and corner.

10.2. Pedraza: Medieval Village Charm

Pedraza, nestled in the province of Segovia, is a picturesque medieval village that captivates visitors with its timeless charm. This walled hamlet, with its cobbled streets and stone houses, offers a glimpse into Spain's rich history and architectural heritage. The village is entered through the Puerta de la Villa, the main gate, which leads into the Plaza Mayor, Pedraza's central square. This beautiful square is surrounded by well-preserved medieval buildings, including the old town hall with its distinctive arcade. The Plaza Mayor is the heart of the village, where locals and visitors gather to enjoy the relaxed atmosphere and the stunning views of the surrounding countryside.

One of the highlights of Pedraza is the Castillo de Pedraza, a fortress that dates back to the 13th century. The castle has been beautifully restored and now houses a museum that showcases a collection of Spanish and European art, including paintings, tapestries, and furniture. The castle also offers panoramic views of the village and the Sierra de Guadarrama mountains. Pedraza is known for its traditional crafts, and visitors can explore artisanal shops selling handmade products such as ceramics, textiles, and wrought ironwork. These shops are scattered throughout the village, providing an opportunity to purchase unique souvenirs and gifts. The village is also famous for its gastronomy, with several restaurants and taverns offering local specialties such as roast lamb, chorizo, and sopa castellana, a traditional garlic soup. Dining in Pedraza is a delightful experience, with many establishments set in historic buildings or offering outdoor seating in the charming streets.

Pedraza hosts several cultural events throughout the year, the most notable being the Noche de las Velas. This magical event takes place on the first two Saturdays of July, when the village is illuminated by thousands of candles, creating an enchanting atmosphere. Concerts and other cultural activities are held during this time, adding to the festive spirit.

In conclusion, Pedraza is a medieval village that offers a serene escape from the hustle and bustle of modern life. Its well-preserved architecture, rich history, and vibrant cultural scene make it a must-visit destination for those exploring the Segovia region. Whether strolling through the cobbled streets, admiring the views from the castle, or savoring the local cuisine, visitors to Pedraza are sure to be charmed by its medieval allure.

10.3. Sierra de Guadarrama National Park

The Sierra de Guadarrama National Park, located in the Segovia province, is a natural haven that offers visitors a chance to immerse themselves in the beauty of the Spanish countryside. This expansive park, which covers over 33,000 hectares, is a part of the larger Sierra de Guadarrama mountain range, which stretches across the central part of the Iberian Peninsula. One of the most striking features of the park is its diverse landscape, which includes rugged peaks, lush pine forests, serene alpine meadows, and crystal-clear streams. The highest peak in the park is Peñalara, which stands at 2,428 meters and offers breathtaking views of the surrounding area. The park's varied terrain provides a habitat for a rich array of flora and fauna, including species such as the Spanish imperial eagle, the Iberian ibex, and the Pyrenean desman.

Visitors to the Sierra de Guadarrama National Park can enjoy a wide range of outdoor activities. Hiking is a popular pastime, with numerous trails that cater to all levels of fitness and experience. The Ruta de las Cascadas, for example, is a scenic trail that takes hikers past a series of beautiful waterfalls. For those interested in mountaineering, the park offers challenging climbs, with routes that lead to the summit of Peñalara and other peaks. In addition to hiking and climbing, the park is also a great destination for birdwatching, as it is home to a variety of bird species, including the black vulture and the common rock thrush. During the winter months, the park's higher elevations become a playground for snow sports, with areas designated for cross-country skiing and snowshoeing.

The park is equipped with visitor centers, such as the Centro de Visitantes Valle de la Fuenfría in Cercedilla and the Centro de Visitantes del Parque Nacional in Rascafría. These centers provide information about the park's trails, wildlife, and conservation efforts. They also offer educational programs and guided tours, which are a great way to learn more about the natural and cultural heritage of the Sierra de Guadarrama.

In conclusion, the Sierra de Guadarrama National Park is a natural treasure that offers visitors a chance to connect with nature and enjoy a wide range of outdoor activities. Whether you're hiking through the forests, climbing the rugged peaks, or simply enjoying the stunning scenery, the park is a must-visit destination for nature lovers and outdoor enthusiasts visiting the Segovia region.

10.4. El Escorial and Valley of the Fallen

El Escorial and the Valley of the Fallen are two significant historical sites located near Segovia, each offering visitors a glimpse into different aspects of Spain's rich history. El Escorial, officially known as the Royal Site of San Lorenzo de El Escorial, is a vast architectural complex that served as a monastery, royal palace, museum, and school. It was commissioned by King Philip II in the 16th century and is a stunning example of Renaissance architecture. The complex is situated in the town of San Lorenzo de El Escorial, about an hour's drive from Segovia. The most notable feature of El Escorial is the Royal Monastery, which houses the Basilica of San Lorenzo, with its impressive dome and altarpiece. The monastery also contains the Royal Pantheon, the burial place of many Spanish kings and queens. Visitors can explore the beautifully decorated rooms, including the library, which holds a priceless collection of manuscripts and books.

El Escorial is also home to a museum that showcases a diverse collection of art, including works by prominent Spanish painters such as El Greco and Velázquez. The complex is surrounded by well-manicured gardens, providing a peaceful setting for a leisurely stroll. The Valley of the Fallen, or Valle de los Caídos, is located about 9 kilometers from El Escorial. This controversial monument was built by the Franco regime to commemorate those who died during the Spanish Civil War. The site features a massive cross, which stands over 150 meters tall, making it one of the world's largest crosses. Beneath the cross is the Basilica of the Holy Cross, carved into the rock of the mountain. The basilica's interior is adorned with mosaics and sculptures, and it serves as the final resting place for Francisco Franco and José Antonio Primo de Rivera, the founder of the Falange movement.

The Valley of the Fallen is set within a beautiful natural landscape, with views of the surrounding Sierra de Guadarrama mountains. While the site is a subject of political controversy, it remains an important part of Spain's history and attracts many visitors each year. In conclusion, El Escorial and the Valley of the Fallen are two significant historical sites near Segovia that offer visitors a chance to explore Spain's rich cultural and political history. From the Renaissance splendor of El Escorial to the solemnity of the Valley of the Fallen, these sites provide a fascinating insight into the country's past.

10.5. Wine Tours in the Ribera del Duero Region

The Ribera del Duero region, located near Segovia, is one of Spain's most prestigious wine-producing areas, renowned for its high-quality red wines. A wine tour in this region offers visitors an opportunity to explore the picturesque vineyards, learn about the winemaking process, and, of course, sample some of the finest wines Spain has to offer. One of the most iconic wineries in the Ribera del Duero region is Bodegas Protos, situated in the town of Peñafiel. This winery, whose name means "first" in Greek, was the first winery established in the region and has been producing wine since 1927.

Bodegas Protos is known for its state-of-the-art facilities, which include an impressive underground cellar designed by the famous architect Richard Rogers. Visitors can take guided tours of the winery, which include a walk through the vineyards, an explanation of the winemaking process, and a tasting of their signature wines.

Another notable winery is Bodegas Vega Sicilia, located in Valbuena de Duero. This winery is one of the oldest and most prestigious in Spain, with a history dating back to 1864. Vega Sicilia is famous for its meticulous winemaking process and its commitment to quality, which is reflected in its highly acclaimed wines. The winery offers private tours by appointment, where visitors can explore the historic cellars, learn about the winery's history, and taste their legendary wines. For those interested in a more intimate wine-tasting experience, Bodegas Arzuaga Navarro in Quintanilla de Onésimo is a family-owned winery that produces a range of exceptional wines. The winery is set in a beautiful location, surrounded by vineyards and pine forests, providing a tranquil setting for wine tasting. Visitors can tour the facilities, including the barrel room and the aging cellar, and enjoy a tasting of their wines, which are known for their elegance and complexity.

In addition to visiting individual wineries, there are several tour companies that offer guided wine tours of the Ribera del Duero region. These tours typically include transportation from Segovia, visits to multiple wineries, wine tastings, and sometimes even lunch at a local restaurant. This is a convenient option for those who want to explore the region's wines without the hassle of driving. In conclusion, a wine tour in the Ribera del Duero region is a must-do experience for wine enthusiasts visiting Segovia. The region's wineries, from historic estates like Bodegas Vega Sicilia to family-run operations like Bodegas Arzuaga Navarro, offer a fascinating glimpse into the world of Spanish winemaking. Whether you're a seasoned wine connoisseur or a casual enthusiast, the Ribera del Duero region has something to delight every palate.

CHAPTER 11

ENTERTAINMENT AND NIGHTLIFE

11.1. Flamenco Shows and Cultural Performances

Segovia, a city rich in history and cultural heritage, offers visitors an array of cultural experiences, including the vibrant and passionate art of flamenco. Flamenco shows in Segovia provide an opportunity to immerse oneself in the soulful music, intricate dance, and emotional intensity that characterize this traditional Spanish art form. One of the popular venues for experiencing flamenco in Segovia is La Cueva de San Esteban, located in the historic Jewish Quarter. This intimate venue, set in a cave-like space, creates a unique and atmospheric setting for flamenco performances. The shows feature talented dancers, guitarists, and singers, who bring the traditional and contemporary styles of flamenco to life. La Cueva de San Esteban also offers a menu of Spanish cuisine, allowing visitors to enjoy a meal while taking in the performance.

Another venue for flamenco and cultural performances is the Palacio de la Floresta, situated near the Alcázar of Segovia. This elegant palace hosts a variety of cultural events, including flamenco shows, classical music concerts, and theatrical performances. The grandeur of the venue adds an extra layer of sophistication to the performances, making it a memorable experience for attendees. For those seeking a more immersive flamenco experience, the Tablao Flamenco El Sitio, located in the heart of Segovia, offers regular flamenco shows featuring skilled artists. The tablao provides an authentic atmosphere, with traditional decor and seating arrangements that allow for an up-close view of the performers. The intensity and emotion of the dancers and musicians create a captivating experience that showcases the depth and beauty of flamenco.

In addition to dedicated flamenco venues, Segovia hosts several cultural festivals throughout the year, where flamenco performances are often featured. The Festival de Segovia, held in the summer, is a celebration of music and arts, with a diverse program that includes flamenco alongside other genres of music and performance arts. In conclusion, Flamenco shows and cultural performances in Segovia offer visitors a chance to experience the rich artistic traditions of Spain. From intimate tablaos to grand palaces, the city provides a variety of settings to enjoy the passionate and soul-stirring art of flamenco. Whether you are a flamenco aficionado or new to the art form, a flamenco show in Segovia is an experience not to be missed.

11.2. Bars and Pubs in the Historic Center

Click on the Link or Scan QR Code with a device to view a comprehensive map of Bars and Pubs in Segovia – https://shorturl.at/hzCK1

Segovia's historic center is not only a treasure trove of architectural wonders but also a vibrant hub of culinary delights and lively nightlife. The city's bars and pubs offer a perfect blend of traditional charm and contemporary flair, providing locals and visitors alike with spaces to unwind, socialize, and savor the local flavors. This essay explores six notable bars and pubs in the historic center of Segovia, highlighting their unique offerings, locations, and the experiences they provide.

Cervecería El Sitio: A Beer Lover's Haven

Located near the iconic Aqueduct, Cervecería El Sitio is a popular spot for beer enthusiasts. Known for its wide selection of local and international beers, this bar offers a cozy atmosphere with rustic decor. The prices are reasonable, with beers starting at around €2.50. In addition to drinks, El Sitio serves delicious tapas and light meals, making it a great place to start your evening in Segovia.

Bar Santana: A Taste of Tradition

Nestled in the heart of the Jewish Quarter, Bar Santana is a charming establishment that exudes a warm, traditional ambiance. Renowned for its vermút (vermouth) and tapas, this bar is a favorite among locals for its authentic Segovian experience. Prices are affordable, with tapas ranging from €1.50 to €3.00. Don't miss the opportunity to try their signature tortilla española (Spanish omelet) and croquetas (croquettes).

La Taberna Rubi: A Wine Connoisseur's Delight
Situated on Calle Infanta Isabel, La Taberna Rubi is a sophisticated wine bar that specializes in regional wines from Ribera del Duero and Rueda. The intimate setting, with its stone walls and wooden barrels, provides an ideal backdrop for wine tasting. Prices for a glass of wine start at around €3.00, and the bar also offers a selection of cheese and charcuterie boards to complement your drink.

El Fogón Sefardí: A Cultural Fusion
El Fogón Sefardí, located near the Plaza Mayor, is a unique bar that combines the flavors of Sephardic cuisine with a modern twist. The bar's decor pays homage to Segovia's Jewish heritage, creating an inviting and culturally rich atmosphere. Prices are mid-range, with specialty cocktails starting at €5.00 and tapas from €3.00. Be sure to try their signature Sephardic pastries and spiced tea.

La Concepción: A Lively Nightspot
Just a stone's throw from the Cathedral, La Concepción is a vibrant bar known for its lively atmosphere and eclectic music selection. This is the place to be if you're looking for a night of dancing and socializing. Drink prices are reasonable, with beers and mixed drinks starting at around €3.00. The bar often hosts live music and DJ sets, adding to the energetic vibe.

Irish Rover: A Touch of Ireland in Segovia
For those seeking a taste of Ireland in Segovia, the Irish Rover is a must-visit. Located on Calle de Cervantes, this Irish pub offers a selection of international beers, whiskeys, and classic pub fare. Prices are slightly higher, with beers starting at €3.50, but the authentic Irish ambiance and friendly staff make it worth the visit. The pub also features live sports screenings and occasional live music events.

The bars and pubs in the historic center of Segovia offer a diverse range of experiences, from traditional tapas bars to modern wine lounges and lively nightspots. Each establishment provides a unique glimpse into the city's culinary and cultural landscape, making them essential stops on any visit to Segovia. Whether you're looking to sample local wines, enjoy live music, or simply soak in the historic ambiance, these bars and pubs promise memorable evenings filled with flavor, fun, and local charm.

11.3. Live Music Venues and Nightclubs

Segovia, a city renowned for its historic charm and cultural richness, also boasts a vibrant nightlife scene that caters to music enthusiasts and party-goers alike. From intimate live music venues to energetic nightclubs, the city offers a variety of settings for an unforgettable night out. This essay delves into six prominent live music venues and nightclubs in Segovia, providing insights into their offerings, locations, and the unique experiences they provide.

La Cárcel: Segovia Centro de Creación

La Cárcel: Segovia Centro de Creación, located in a former prison, is a unique cultural space that hosts an array of live music events, from jazz concerts to indie rock performances. The venue's atmospheric setting, with its historical architecture, adds a distinctive charm to the musical experience. Prices for events vary, with tickets typically ranging from €10 to €20. Visitors are advised to check the venue's schedule in advance and arrive early to secure good seats.

Beat Club Segovia

Beat Club Segovia, situated near the Aqueduct, is a popular nightclub known for its lively ambiance and diverse music programming. The club features live DJ sets, themed parties, and occasional live band performances, covering genres from electronic dance music to pop and rock. Entry fees vary depending on the event, usually around €5 to €10, with drink prices being reasonably affordable. The club's energetic atmosphere makes it a favorite among young locals and tourists looking to dance the night away.

Sala Boss

Sala Boss, located on Calle de los Coches, is a versatile venue that hosts live music performances, DJ nights, and private events. The space is known for its cozy interior and quality sound system, providing an intimate setting for enjoying live bands and singers. Cover charges and drink prices are moderate, making it an accessible option for a night out. The venue's diverse music lineup appeals to a wide range of tastes, from rock and pop to Latin and reggae.

Bar Santana

Bar Santana, nestled in the historic Jewish Quarter, is a charming bar that occasionally features live music performances, including flamenco shows and acoustic sets. The bar's rustic decor and warm atmosphere create a perfect backdrop for enjoying music over a glass of wine or a cold beer. Prices are affordable, with no cover charge for most music events. It's a great spot for those seeking a laid-back evening with a touch of local culture.

Discoteca La Luna

Discoteca La Luna, situated on Avenida del Padre Claret, is a nightclub that offers a vibrant party scene with a mix of live music and DJ sets. The club's spacious dance floor and modern lighting make it a popular destination for night owls. Entry fees are typically around €10, which often includes a complimentary drink. The club's varied music programming caters to different tastes, ensuring a lively and enjoyable night for all attendees.

Pub Irlandés Daniel's

Pub Irlandés Daniel's, located on Calle de San Juan, is an Irish pub that frequently hosts live music nights, featuring local bands and solo artists. The pub's cozy ambiance, coupled with its selection of beers and whiskies, provides a comfortable setting for enjoying music. There's usually no cover charge, making it an affordable option for a casual night out. The pub's friendly vibe and live performances make it a favorite among locals and visitors looking for a relaxed musical experience.

Segovia's live music venues and nightclubs offer a diverse array of options for experiencing the city's nightlife. From historic spaces hosting jazz concerts to modern clubs with energetic dance floors, there's something for every music lover and party-goer. Whether you're in the mood for an intimate live performance, a flamenco show, or a night of dancing, Segovia's nightlife scene promises memorable moments filled with rhythm, melody, and fun.

11.4. Theatres and Cinemas

Segovia, a city celebrated for its historical and cultural richness, also boasts a vibrant arts scene with a variety of theatres and cinemas. From traditional performances in historic venues to contemporary films in modern cinemas, Segovia offers a range of entertainment options for locals and visitors alike. This essay explores six notable theatres and cinemas in Segovia, highlighting their unique features, locations, and the experiences they provide.

Teatro Juan Bravo: A Cultural Landmark

Located in the heart of Segovia on Plaza Mayor, Teatro Juan Bravo is a historic theatre that serves as a cultural hub for the city. The theatre hosts a diverse array of performances, including plays, concerts, dance shows, and operas. With its elegant architecture and intimate setting, Teatro Juan Bravo offers a memorable experience for theatre enthusiasts. Ticket prices vary depending on the event, typically ranging from €10 to €30. Visitors are advised to book tickets in advance and arrive early to enjoy the beautiful interior of the theatre.

Cine Artesiete Segovia: A Modern Cinematic Experience

Cine Artesiete Segovia, situated in the Luz de Castilla shopping center, is a contemporary cinema that screens the latest national and international films. The cinema features state-of-the-art sound and projection technology, ensuring a high-quality viewing experience. Ticket prices are around €8, with discounts available for students, seniors, and on certain days of the week. The cinema's location within the shopping center makes it convenient to combine a movie with shopping or dining.

Sala Ex.Presa: An Intimate Venue for the Arts

Sala Ex.Presa, located in La Cárcel_Segovia Centro de Creación, is an intimate venue that hosts a variety of artistic events, including small-scale theatre productions, independent film screenings, and cultural workshops. The space is known for its cozy atmosphere and support for emerging artists. Ticket prices are affordable, usually under €10, making it an accessible option for experiencing local arts and culture.

Palacio de Quintanar: A Historic Setting for Events

Palacio de Quintanar, a Renaissance palace, serves as a multi-functional space for cultural events, including theatre performances, film screenings, and art exhibitions. The palace's stunning architecture and historical significance add a unique dimension to the events held here. Prices for events vary, with many exhibitions offering free entry. The palace's central location near the Aqueduct makes it easily accessible for visitors.

CineBox Plaza de Armas: A Cozy Cinema Experience

CineBox Plaza de Armas is a small cinema located near the Plaza de Armas shopping center. The cinema offers a selection of mainstream and independent films in a cozy setting. Ticket prices are similar to those of Cine Artesiete Segovia, with discounts available on certain days. The cinema's intimate size provides a comfortable and personal viewing experience, making it a favorite among locals.

Teatro Paladio: A Space for Inclusive Arts

Teatro Paladio, situated on Calle de San Nicolás, is a unique theatre that focuses on inclusive arts, providing a platform for performances by artists with disabilities. The theatre hosts a variety of shows, including plays, dance performances, and music concerts, with an emphasis on promoting social inclusion through the arts. Ticket prices are generally affordable, and the theatre's welcoming atmosphere makes it a special place to experience the power of inclusive artistry.

Segovia's theatres and cinemas offer a window into the city's vibrant arts scene, providing entertainment options that cater to a wide range of tastes and interests. From historic venues hosting classical performances to modern cinemas screening the latest films, Segovia's stage and screen scene is a testament to the city's cultural diversity and artistic vitality. Whether you're a theatre aficionado, a film buff, or simply looking for an enjoyable evening out, Segovia's theatres and cinemas promise memorable experiences that enrich your visit to this enchanting city.

11.5. Seasonal Festivals and Outdoor Events

Segovia, a city rich in history and culture, comes alive with a variety of seasonal festivals and outdoor events throughout the year. These celebrations showcase the city's traditions, gastronomy, and artistic talent, providing visitors with unique and memorable experiences. One of the most iconic festivals in Segovia is the Fiesta de San Juan y San Pedro, which takes place in late June. This festival marks the start of summer and is celebrated with a series of events, including open-air concerts, traditional dances, and sports competitions. The highlight of the festival is the procession of the giants and bigheads, colorful figures that parade through the streets, delighting both children and adults.

In September, Segovia hosts the Hay Festival, an international literary and arts festival that attracts writers, artists, and intellectuals from around the world. The festival features a diverse program of talks, readings, and performances, held in various historic venues throughout the city. The Hay Festival provides a platform for cultural exchange and intellectual discussion, making it a must-attend event for literature and arts enthusiasts. The Noche de San Juan celebrated on the night of June 23rd, is a magical event that marks the summer solstice. The city comes alive with bonfires, music, and dancing, as locals and visitors gather to celebrate the longest day of the year. The tradition of jumping over the bonfires is believed to bring good luck and purification.

In October, Segovia celebrates its Patron Saint Festival in honor of San Frutos, the patron saint of the city. The festival includes religious processions, concerts, and a variety of cultural activities. One of the most anticipated events is the Alcaldada, a medieval reenactment that takes place in the Plaza Mayor, where actors dressed in period costumes recreate scenes from Segovia's history.

For food lovers, the Titirimundi International Puppet Festival in May transforms Segovia into a vibrant stage for puppetry and street theater. Performers from around the globe bring their unique puppet shows to the city, delighting audiences of all ages. The festival's lively atmosphere is complemented by street performers and food stalls, making it a festive experience for the whole family.

In summary, Segovia's seasonal festivals and outdoor events offer a rich tapestry of experiences that reflect the city's cultural heritage and vibrant community spirit. From literary gatherings and medieval reenactments to summer solstice celebrations and puppetry, these festivities provide visitors with a glimpse into the traditions and artistic expressions of this enchanting city. Whether you're a history buff, a food enthusiast, or an art lover, Segovia's festivals and events are sure to leave a lasting impression.

CONCLUSION AND INSIDER TIPS FOR VISITORS

As we draw to a close on our journey through the pages of the Segovia Comprehensive Guide, I hope that the rich tapestry of history, culture, and culinary delights woven throughout this guide has ignited a spark of curiosity and wanderlust in your heart. Segovia, with its ancient stones whispering tales of yore and its vibrant present pulsating with life, is a city that beckons to be explored, experienced, and cherished. Here are some recommendations and insider tips;

Embrace the Pace

Segovia invites you to slow down and savor each moment. Allow yourself to be captivated by the intricate details of its architecture, the subtle flavors of its cuisine, and the warmth of its people. Wander through its streets without haste, for the true essence of Segovia is found in the leisurely exploration of its nooks and crannies.

Engage with the Locals

The soul of Segovia lies in its inhabitants. Engage with the locals, whether it's exchanging pleasantries with a shopkeeper or sharing a laugh with fellow diners at a tapas bar. Their stories and insights will enrich your understanding of the city and make your experience more authentic and memorable.

Delve into History

Segovia is a living museum, and each of its landmarks tells a chapter of its storied past. Don't just admire the Aqueduct, Alcázar, and Cathedral for their architectural beauty; seek out their histories and the roles they played in shaping Segovia. This deeper appreciation will transform your visit into a journey through time.

Savor the Flavors

The gastronomy of Segovia is an integral part of its identity. Indulge in traditional dishes like cochinillo asado and judiones de La Granja, but also be open to contemporary interpretations of these classics. Visit local markets, sample products, and perhaps even take a cooking class to bring a taste of Segovia back home with you.

Celebrate the Festivals

If your visit coincides with one of Segovia's many festivals, immerse yourself in the celebrations. Whether it's the solemnity of Holy Week, the joyousness of the Titirimundi Puppet Festival, or the lively atmosphere of the San Juan and San Pedro Fiestas, participating in these events will provide a unique glimpse into the city's cultural heart.

Venture Beyond

While the historic center of Segovia is undoubtedly enchanting, don't miss the opportunity to explore its surroundings. The Romanesque churches dotting the countryside, the Royal Palace of La Granja de San Ildefonso, and the natural beauty of the Sierra de Guadarrama are all within easy reach and add depth to your Segovian experience.

Insider Tips

1. Sunset at the Alcázar: For a magical view, visit the Alcázar of Segovia at sunset. The changing colors of the sky provide a stunning backdrop to this fairy-tale castle.

2. Aqueduct at Night: The Roman Aqueduct takes on a different character at night when it's beautifully illuminated. A nighttime stroll here is both romantic and awe-inspiring.

3. Hidden Courtyards: Segovia is full of hidden courtyards and gardens. Take a detour down a quiet street or follow a seemingly inconspicuous alley to discover these peaceful retreats.

4. Local Pastries: Don't leave Segovia without trying the local pastries, such as ponche segoviano and rosquillas de yema. They're perfect souvenirs to satisfy your sweet tooth back home.

5. Avoid Peak Hours: To enjoy a more tranquil visit to popular attractions like the Cathedral and Alcázar, try to visit early in the morning or later in the afternoon to avoid crowds.

6. Guided Tours: Consider taking a guided tour for a more in-depth understanding of Segovia's history and culture. Many guides are locals who provide fascinating insights and anecdotes.

In conclusion, Segovia is a city that promises an unforgettable journey for those willing to delve into its depths. It's a place where history is not just remembered; it's felt. Where every meal is a celebration of tradition, and every street corner tells a story. As you turn the pages of this guide and embark on your exploration of Segovia, may you discover not just the beauty of a city but the essence of a timeless legacy. And may your memories of Segovia be as enduring as the stones of its ancient aqueduct.

SEGOVIA TRAVEL PLANNER

NAME:
_____

DEPARTURE DATE:
_____

RETURN DATE:
_____

MY PACKING LIST

- _____
- _____
- _____
- _____
- _____
- _____
- _____
- _____
- _____
- _____
- _____

MY TRAVEL BUDGET

A-7 DAY TRAVEL ITINERARIES PLANNING

DAY 1:

DAY 2:

DAY 3:

DAY 4:

DAY 5:

DAY 6:

DAY 7

MUST-DO THINGS IN SEGOVIA

-
-
-
-
-
-
-
-
-
-
-
-
-
-
-
-

MUST-TRY FOOD IN SEGOVIA

LIST OF TOURIST SITES & HIDDEN GEMS TO VISIT IN SEGOVIA

-
-
-
-
-
-
-
-
-
-
-
-
-
-

SHARE YOUR SEGOVIA TRAVEL EXPERIENCE

Printed in Great Britain
by Amazon